To

Sid & Helen

Trojans Forever

[signature]

[signature] 93' Fight on!

CONQ

A Cavalcade of USC Football

QUEST

John Robinson
and Joe Jares

Arthur Neff Publishing

Santa Monica, California
London, England

Dedication

To each young man who has worn the Trojan uniform and contributed so much to the 'Spirit of Troy.'

John Robinson

First Edition 1981

Printed in the United States of America
Library of Congress Catalog Card Number 81-82627
International Standard Book Number 0-940396-00-9

Project Director: David Boss
Designer: Bruce Claypool
Production Manager: Robert Wenkam
Page Mechanicals: The Drawing Room
Color Separations: Color Graphics
Printing and Binding: Kingsport Press

CONTENTS

INTRODUCTION

When you're a kid, you usually have some local teams you cheer for, but you're also well aware of the nation's elite teams: the New York Yankees, the Green Bay Packers in the Vince Lombardi era, the Boston Celtics led by Bill Russell. I put the USC and Notre Dame football teams in that category. USC has always had that fantasy thing going for it with kids, and adult fans, too. If you live in America and decide to root for a team — not because it plays nearby but just because it's excellent or colorful — the Trojans could easily be your choice. USC has a national following, a special status.

People in Connecticut and Georgia know the Trojans because of the succession of great tailbacks and from the Rose Bowl games and the nationally televised battles with UCLA and Notre Dame. USC's record in big TV games is phenomenal.

When I was growing up in the Bay Area, I was aware of USC, all right, but my heroes were the San Francisco 49ers and a minor-league baseball team, the Oakland Oaks. I was a Cal football fan, too, because of Johnny Olszewski, Pete Schabarum and the other stars on the teams coached by Pappy Waldorf. As a high school football player, I can remember eliminating USC from any serious consideration. It was beyond what I saw myself aspiring to.

I went to Oregon, and the first varsity game I ever played was against USC. It was also the first time I'd ever seen the Coliseum. I played, oh, the last two minutes of the ballgame, and I can remember coming out of the huddle and lining up against Chuck Griffith, 6-6, 239, and Leon Clarke, 6-4, 210, one behind the other. I couldn't see anything other than those two guys looking at me, and those crimson red helmets. It may be fantasy, but I'm sure I remember one of them saying to the other, "Look what we got here." I think I was offsides by about two counts, being so nervous.

When I became an assistant coach at Oregon there still was a feeling of awe, but there was a great affection for USC, too, because an Oregon man, John McKay, was coaching there. USC was the standard you set your goals by. We would tell our kids, "These people are the best. You're playing the best football team, maybe the best you'll ever play against."

I was a defensive coach when we played against O.J. Simpson two years in a row. Those were *monumental* days for us, and we did well against him, holding him to 65 and 60 yards in the two years. Other than Notre Dame, I think Oregon did the best job on Simpson. I can remember staying up all night a couple of times just working on it, trying to come up with a plan to stop him. Those games were two of the most memorable of my life, but USC was looking ahead, thinking of somebody else, I'm sure.

There is no question that almost every team raises its level of play when it goes against USC. I think one of the reasons USC does so well in clutch circumstances is that the other side, playing on so much emotion and actually having a chance to win near the end, stops and says, "Oh, my God!," and blinks at the critical moment.

Getting jacked up to play the Trojans ran contrary to our best interests at Oregon. We often played great against USC, then lost by a close margin. Sometimes we'd even win and then have a terrible time getting our feet back on the ground. I can remember beating USC once and losing to San Jose State the next week.

I was an assistant up in Eugene for 12 years. In 1972 our program was staggering badly and I was anxious to move. It was obviously a pivotal point in my coaching career when McKay, who had been an Oregon assistant coach when I was a player, hired me to join his staff. I couldn't have picked a better year to become a Trojan.

The image of USC is that it has all the talent. Mike Garretts and Ricky Bells designed by the School of Engineering and mass produced by the School of Medicine. I expected all the players to be as tall as Chuck Griffith and Leon Clarke. But when I got there, I was more impressed with the players' attitude and competitiveness than with their talent or size. The most dramatic difference I saw between the men at USC and the ones I had dealt with was that competitiveness, that concentration or focus on what they wanted to do, which was win. That's the thing that maintains traditions at successful places: an attitude that runs through the coach and player, runs through the alum, runs through the fan. It's a belief system that comes on you, and you in fact become part of *it*.

Of course, USC works hard to recruit great athletes. But just assemble talent without the belief system and your program will crumble. I felt right away that we were going to win, no matter what. The feeling in the air was, "Find out what we have to do, then get going and *do* it."

I walked into maybe one of the best football teams of all time in 1972. The players were highly motivated because they had been unsuccessful in 1970 and 1971, 6-4-1 both years. That team became unified and played with great enthusiasm — Mike Rae, Anthony Davis, Sam Cunningham,

Two decades of USC head football coaches — John Robinson and John McKay — study the action from the sidelines.

Lynn Swann, Charles Young. They really were never pressed all season.

After three years as an assistant to McKay — I felt I learned more from him than any man — I moved to the Oakland Raiders to coach under my boyhood friend, John Madden. I loved it there, partly because the Raiders worked very hard and had a lot of those belief systems that USC has.

When McKay's decision to leave became known in 1975, the season wasn't over yet. I got a call from John Hubbard, the president of USC. He was at the airport in Washington, D.C. He said, "Do you want a job?" I said, "Yeah." He said, "Well, you got it." And that was it. It was a short conversation.

There were concerns in some quarters about my following a legend, McKay. But USC still had the belief system, the attitude. I think a good definition of tradition is an organization that's more important than the individuals in it. The organization outlasts individuals. John McKay left me fine players and a winning tradition when he went off to the National Football League. (A *Sports Illustrated* writer at the time came up with an apocryphal bumper sticker: "God Isn't Dead; He Just Moved to Tampa.")

Part of the tradition was the love of big games. Coach McKay had a great love for them and was always at his best for them. The feeling filtered down to the assistants and players. There was not a lot of talk. There was almost a quiet on our practice field and a gleam in everybody's eye. I never saw us worried. I've never been worried going into a big game with a USC football team.

People choose this university because USC is a winner — and we recruit that way. We don't get many insecure players. We tell them, "You have a chance to belong to a school, to a football team, that is second to none." When you talk to a young man about going to USC, you're dealing with one of his dreams, one of his fantasies. It's an incredible opportunity for him.

I said when I came back from pro football that I had missed the Trojan horse, Traveler, and I was only half-kidding. The hoopla, the rah-rah stuff, is another wonderful part of it. The horse, the band, the song girls — there's a delightful aura around college football. It's unique. Believe it or not, I'm conscious of the horse in the Coliseum. I always look for him in the tunnel before, and during the game I take pleasure in seeing

him come galloping around the track while the band plays *Conquest.*

And I love the band, which has become very close to our team. Back in my first year we lost horribly the first week to Missouri. One headline in a paper said, "How can a guy ruin a program so fast?" Steve Harvey, the USC School of Journalism alumnus who writes *The Bottom Ten,* picked us as the worst team in the nation that week.

We were to play Oregon the following weekend, and the band came out on the practice field Thursday and played. Just came out on its own. One little coed — I think she played the clarinet — put down her instrument, ran over and grabbed one of our players and asked him to dance. So they started dancing.

That got to be a steady routine, and we won all the rest of our games and went on to the Rose Bowl. The day before the Rose Bowl, in pouring-down rain, the band was practicing near us and refused to go in until it could play for the team. We stood out in the downpour and had our little rally. (Lynn Swann, our great wide receiver of the early 1970s, used to come off the field in a game and every once in a while run over and *lead* the band. That was only fair, I guess, because back in the 1940s, Tommy Walker used to come out of the band to kick USC's extra points.)

We open spring drills and game-preparation practices to everybody on campus. I like the idea of people looking at our team and feeling that it belongs to them. The team doesn't belong to me, and it doesn't belong to the athletic department. It belongs to the people of USC — the students, the alumni, the people who care.

One of the great things about USC is its diversity. There is a genuine interest in the football team *and* the total university. This place has turned out columnist Art Buchwald, George Lucas, the man who made *Star Wars,* and singer Marilyn Horne — as well as O.J. Simpson. People can learn how to play left tackle or the cello. I'm proud that USC has had more NCAA postgraduate scholarship winners than any other university. Brad Budde, Paul McDonald, and Gordon Adams are the most recent of 12 football players who have earned the honor since 1965. And Pat Haden in 1974 also won a Rhodes Scholarship.

There is a genuine interest in the football team

and the total university. Football is almost like bait for us; it gets the fans hooked and soon thereafter, many people find themselves drawn into other areas of interest on our campus.

It certainly has happened to my family. Barbara, my wife, is a student in Music and together, we are heavily involved contributors and fund raisers for the School of Performing Arts.

There are friendships at USC and loyalties to this school that amaze me, and being part of it I consider one of the real privileges of my life. There's a great tradition, and it's not just athletics. But I do feel, as ex-USC President John Hubbard has said, "Sometimes football is the glue that holds all of that tradition together."

I hope this book reflects the spirit, fun, and excitement that have come with the victories (and yes, defeats) in more than 90 years of USC football.

John Robinson
July, 1981

The Trojans squad celebrates in front of the rooting section after the 1979 thrashing of UCLA 49-14. John Robinson hugs senior tailback Charles White, who rushed for almost 200 yards.

He

ritage

Elmer C. (Gloomy Gus) Henderson

USC football started in 1888, eight years after the school was founded and 14 years after the first intercollegiate game (Harvard versus McGill, 1874, although some historians claim it was Princeton versus Rutgers, 1869). The first USC team — John Norton, Harvey Bailey, Will Whitcomb, Ed Young, E.E. Hall, Henry Lillie, E.E. Reed, C.C. Carpenter, F.E. Davis, Arthur Carroll, and Frank N. Lapham — played two games against the Alliance Athletic Club and won both.

Los Angeles was a relatively small town then, maybe not the "sleepy pueblo" described in a school history published in 1939 but certainly no bustling, smoggy metropolis. USC was a small college out in the middle of the mustard fields, and students traveled to and from their homes in streetcars, sometimes shooting at rabbits from the rear platforms.

The football played at first was at a high school or small-college level. In fact, in the early days USC had a 4-3-3 record against Los Angeles High School, 12-1-1 against Caltech, 16-5-2 against Occidental College, and 13-4-4 versus its biggest rival of the era, Pomona College. (An early heroic feat: Elwyn Caley's 107-yard kickoff return against Pomona in 1902, is still in the record book. The field then was 110 yards long.) Other notable opponents were the Whittier Reform School, Loyola, Orange Athletic Club, and the Perris Indians.

Coaching wasn't too important. There was no coach at all for 10 seasons and in 1901 the coach for the one-game season (a 6-0 loss to Pomona) was law professor Clair Tappaan, whose son Francis was an All-America end almost three decades later. Dean Cromwell, famous as track & field's "maker of champions," was head football coach for five seasons and had a 21-8-6 record; Harvey Holmes was 19-5-3 in four seasons.

There were few if any O.J. Simpson-caliber athletes on those teams, but the players were interesting nevertheless. Frank (Rabbit) Malette, captain and quarterback in 1917, weighed only 132 pounds. Ralph Avery, who lettered in 1896 and 1897, became a dentist; one of his descendants graduated from USC in 1981. Tully Knoles, a teammate of Caley's in 1902, was also student body president and later became president of College of the Pacific (COP) in Stockton. Hugh Baillie played in the first USC-Stanford game in 1905, won by Stanford 16-0; he later became a well known reporter and the president of United Press International.

The teams were not nicknamed Trojans from the beginning. USC, like Syracuse and Northwestern, was founded as a Methodist school but later became nondenominational. Its early athletes were known as Methodists or Wesleyans. Before a USC-Stanford track meet, sports writer Owen Bird of the *Los Angeles Times* called attention to the team's fighting spirit and named them Trojans. The name stuck. The date of Bird's article: February 24, 1912.

Not only was the nickname not coined during football season, there *was* no football season at USC in 1912, or 1911 or 1913 either. The fall contact sport was rugby.

The famous bronze statue of The Trojan ("faithful, scholarly, skillful, courageous, ambitious," it says on the concrete base) was unveiled 18 years later, on June 6, 1930, as part of the university's golden anniversary. Football indirectly footed the $10,000 bill, because a one dollar surcharge had been tacked onto alumni season tickets for two years. The sculptor was Roger Noble Burnham, who also did the statue of General Douglas MacArthur which stands in MacArthur Park. Burnham's model for the Trojan warrior was Russ Saunders, who had scored 14 touchdowns for USC in 1929 and passed for three touchdowns in the 1930 Rose Bowl upset of Pitt.

Trojan football hit the big time with the arrival of bespectacled Elmer C. (Gus) Henderson in 1919. A graduate of Oberlin College in his hometown of Oberlin, Ohio, he had a successful coaching career at Broadway High School in Seattle before USC hired him. Fans enjoyed his wide-open game and he had the respect of his players.

"He put the Trojans on the map," said one of his star backs, Gordon Campbell. "He was a great coach when we needed one most, because we were just growing up."

"Not only was he a great coach, but he was a wonderful man," said Brice Taylor, USC's first All-America and also from Seattle. "He was real people.

"You know, I'll never forget the day I was standing on a corner, shivering, because it was cold, and Gus drives by in his car. He sees me, stops and backs up, and says, 'What's the matter, Brice, are you cold?'

"And I said, 'I sure am, coach.' So he reaches into the back seat, takes out his brand new, blue chesterfield coat and says, 'Here, take this, it's yours.'

"You know, years after I left SC, when I was teaching in the South, I was still wearing that coat."

Henderson was usually a pessimist, which led *Times* sports writer Paul Lowry to nickname him Gloomy Gus, after a comic-strip character of the day. Henderson didn't swear and, according to Taylor, "hired an assistant to do the cussing for him. Honest. So, whenever he got to the boiling point, he'd just call on his assistant, and he'd pour it to us."

Henderson was a winner right away: 4-1 in 1919 and 6-0 in 1920. Alumni boosters gave him a Cole automobile in 1923. And it was Henderson who brought in fellow Oberlin man Willis O. Hunter, who became USC's athletic director in 1925 and held the job 32 years.

The present Rose Bowl stadium in Pasadena's Arroyo Seco was built in 1922 — in the shape of a horseshoe. It wasn't expanded into a bowl until six years later. In October of 1922, USC played the first football game in the new structure, a 12-0 loss to Cal (Henderson failed to beat the Bears in five tries). The Tournament of Roses Committee picked Penn State and Cal to play in the 1923 New Year's Day game, but Cal refused the invitation. USC, with an 8-1 season record (9-1 if you count a victory over an alumni team), was the substitute choice.

The Penn State bus was caught in traffic and showed up late for the game, which was eventually finished in near darkness. Henderson was furious, thinking that Nittany Lion Coach Hugo Bezdek had purposely stalled so that (a) the waiting Trojans would get edgy and (b) the game would be played in cooler temperatures. When Penn State arrived, Henderson was there to make his angry charges. Bezdek in turn challenged Gloomy Gus to take off his glasses and fight. Henderson backed down.

"I had just climbed out of bed with the flu and could hardly stand up," said Henderson later. "Also, I knew Bezdek had earned his way through the University of Chicago fighting as a pro under an assumed name, so I decided it would be wiser if the two teams decided the issue."

Brice Taylor, first USC All-America, 1925

18

That decision went to USC 14-3, behind the running of Campbell and Roy (Bullet) Baker and the blocking of Howard (Hobo) Kincaid, not to mention a strong defense. There were two crazy plays in the game. In the first, when USC had possession on the Penn State one, Lowell Lindley's snap went in the wrong direction. It was supposed to go almost parallel to the line to a back lined up on the right, but as Gus explained later in the *Los Angeles Examiner,* "as our line heaved forward, the pigskin hit someone's heel and careened over the Penn State goal line." The play resulted in a Penn State touchback rather than the expected Trojan touchdown.

The second oddball play helped USC — Bezdek later said the luckier team won, not the better team. Howard Galloway was stretched out on the turf at the two-yard line when Bullet Baker's pass, far from the intended receiver, fell in his arms.

According to Rube Samuelsen, who covered the New Year's Day games for many years for the *Pasadena Star-News,* the opposing coaches were still bitter after the game.

Henderson: "The best team won! Good coaching, like the effect of cigarettes, always tells in the long run. It is my personal belief that USC should have won by four more touchdowns. Thank God for the guy who made it a criminal offense to hit a man wearing glasses. Hugo Bezdek is no gentleman."

Bezdek: "The best team lost! A football team with the best coaching in the world could not win against the luck the Trojans had. When playing at its best, my team could beat USC by 40 points. My only wish is that Elmer Henderson had left his glasses home."

It sounded a bit phony, as if Elmer and Hugo were trying, in the manner Muhammad Ali used effectively much later, to build up the gate for a rematch. But there was no rematch. USC never played Penn State again.

The Trojans under Henderson also played the first football game in the Los Angeles Coliseum, a 23-7 win over Pomona on October 6, 1923. (USC played baseball there in 1923 and 1924, more than 30 years before the Dodgers arrived from Brooklyn and used it while Dodger Stadium was under construction.) The Coliseum was built in 1923 in Exposition Park, conveniently next door to the USC campus, at no cost to the taxpayers.

The Community Development Association, a committee of city leaders, borrowed money from 14 banks and built the 75,000-seat stadium for $954,872.98, which would just about pay for a bank of lights today. In 1931, just before the Los Angeles Olympiad, the seating was increased to 101,574.

After compiling a 9-2 record in 1924 and an impressive .865 winning percentage overall, Gloomy Gus was forced out at USC. The reason, according to oldtime Los Angeles sports writer Sid Ziff: Cal and Stanford broke off relations with USC (or threatened to) because of what they charged were under-the-table dealings and over-aggressive recruiting by the Trojan coach.

"That was really a joke," said quarterback Chet Dolley, "because the university didn't have a dime. He made his players responsible for bringing in athletes. I came from Long Beach, so I was assigned to that area. So, naturally, I was in charge of getting Morley Drury."

Drury, Mort Kaer, Brice Taylor, and other Henderson recruits went on to prosper under Howard Jones. Henderson coached the University of Tulsa for 11 years, then coached the Los Angeles Bulldogs, Detroit Lions, and Occidental before retiring from coaching in 1941. He died in 1965 in Palm Springs at the age of 76. In the peristyle end of the Coliseum there is a plaque dedicated to his memory which describes him as "A courageous competitor who inspired his men to fight like Trojans."

Howard Jones, like Henderson, was an Ohioan, born in Excello and reared in Middletown. His brother, Thomas Albert Dwight (Tad) Jones, was a year and a half younger, but they were teammates and classmates at Middletown High, Exeter, and Yale. Howard was a pitcher and end for three years at Yale; Tad was an All-America back in 1907.

Jones had been a head football coach for 13 seasons before he arrived at USC. In 1909 he had enjoyed an unbeaten, unscored-upon season at his alma mater. His Iowa Hawkeyes had won the Big Ten championship in 1921 and ended Notre Dame's unbeaten streak at 22 games. He had also coached at Syracuse, Ohio State, and Duke.

There was little razzle-dazzle to his single-wing football and none to his personality. Neither jokes nor passes were flying about a Jones practice field. The men who played for him are unani-

Enlargement of the Coliseum for the 1932 Olympic Games is in evidence as USC defeats Cal, 6-0, in 1931.

mous in recalling that games on Saturdays were like PTA teas compared to his practices. They are also unanimous in recalling him as stern and taciturn. He smiled about as often as the faces on Mount Rushmore. No USC player was allowed in a poolroom because "the air in such places is usually bad and his associates are not always the best." He didn't even approve of dancing, because it "breaks in on sleeping and eating."

Sometimes sleeping and eating didn't break in on football with Jones. He was known to play golf for small stakes, kibitz at a bridge game or go fishing in the High Sierra, but his world was usually limited to the confines of a gridiron, much as a chess master lives a mental life on the checkered board.

"If there ever was a guy who lived for football," said ex-tackle Ray George, "it was Howard Jones. Every once in a while he would give me a ride back from spring practice at the Coliseum, and we'd get involved in talking football and he'd take his hands off the wheel!"

"He was so engrossed in football that you would pass him on campus and say hello, and he wouldn't notice you," said Cotton Warburton. "You would go to his home, and immediately the furniture would be set up on offense and defense."

"To him, football was the first bright rays of dawn, the noonday sky, and the stars that shine by night," wrote columnist Maxwell Stiles.

That USC teams didn't pass much wasn't entirely because of Jones' conservatism or lack of imagination. The rules of the day favored a running team.

"In those days you had to throw a pass from five yards behind the line of scrimmage," recalled Nick Pappas, the leading rusher in 1935. "If you threw two incomplete passes on the same series of downs, you'd get a five-yard penalty and, if you threw an incomplete pass over the goal line, regardless of the down, the ball went over to the other team just like a touchback."

Thus the Trojan attack featured talented players knocking people down and talented players dodging and darting through, or running over, the bodies. For many of Jones' seasons, it seemed all he had to do was reach into the Sigma Chi house and pluck another superb player from some upper bunk (for many years the Sigma Chis at USC could brag that they had had more All-America football players than UCLA). Jones'

Howard Jones

power running attack and numerous outstanding players gave rise to the nickname The Thundering Herd.

He insisted on precision. "When he told you to get 4½ yards behind center, you got *exactly* 4½ yards," said Warburton. "When he told you to hit a certain hole, you hit that hole. It was all timed that it would open up." But he could be clever, too. He devised an end-around play that led to Ray Sparling averaging 8.5 yards a carry in 1930, 1931, and 1932.

USC football had relatively little competition for the sports fan's dollar and attention in those days. UCLA athletics were in their infancy, and there were no Dodgers, Angels, Rams, Lakers, or Kings. No television and no Disneyland. No Sports Arena, Pauley Pavilion, Dodger Stadium, Anaheim Stadium, or Forum. Jones was *the* big sports figure in town.

Kids grew up dreaming about one day playing for him in the Coliseum. And while they were waiting to grow up, they could play *The Howard Jones Collegiate Football Game* on their dining-room tables at home. (At least three of the boxed games still exist, more than 50 years after they were manufactured. Trojan alumnus Robert Bennra of La Canada has one autographed by Johnny Baker and Erny Pinckert.)

Jones is credited with inventing the all-white T-shirt. According to Beth Ann Krier in the *Los Angeles Times,* the coach "was looking for something lightweight and absorbent his players could wear under their shoulder pads and got the Jockey Menswear Co. to develop a sleeved athletic shirt for him. A year later it went on the market and has since accounted for twice as many annual sales as the old tank-style shirts."

"From 1928 to 1942 I was director of the USC Athletic News Service," said Al Wesson, now retired and living in Lake San Marcos, California. "Naturally, one of my principal — and most enjoyable — objectives was to promote Jones and Trojan football. Since I was a one-man department and my office in the old Student Union building was next to that of Athletic Director Bill Hunter, where Jones hung out (he didn't have an office of his own and it never occurred to him to have one, or that he might need one), there was very close contact between us over a period of 13 years.

"This, I'm happy to say, resulted in a close

Mort Kaer, All-America back, 1926

friendship with The Headman, who was not really an individual inclined to warm relationships. Until his son, Clark, was experienced enough to do it, I wrote Howard's articles for the Christy Walsh Syndicate (which also featured ghost-written pieces by Babe Ruth). Also, he depended upon me to handle much of his quotes for newspaper and radio men and to answer nearly all of his correspondence concerning football.

"Since Howard's hobby outside of football was golf, eventually one of my informal duties developed into setting up his games. This was delightful for me, because since I set 'em up, I usually was a member of the foursome that often included visiting coaches and visiting newspapermen such as Grantland Rice, as well as Howard's local regulars, among the most prominent being Braven Dyer of the *Los Angeles Times*.

"Because Howard couldn't stand my slice, only under the rarest of occasions would he have me as a partner, but he heartily enjoyed playing against me and ribbing me on my bad shots, which gave him plenty of ribbing time."

Like Gloomy Gus, Jones was a winner right away: 11-2 in 1925, 8-2 in 1926 (when the Notre Dame series started with a 13-12 loss), 8-1-1 in 1927. Starting in 1928 he beat Stanford five straight times, and "Pop" Warner departed The Farm. Henderson leftovers helped: Brice Taylor, fast enough to be a back but forced to play in the line because of a deformed left hand, made All-America guard in 1925 (Taylor was black; it wasn't until 39 years later that a second black Trojan, Mike Garrett, made All-America). In 1926 the honor went to running back Mort Kaer, a world-class hurdler. Jones was to coach 18 first-team All-Americas at USC, and probably 10 to 20 others who deserved it just as much, players such as Russ Saunders, Red Badgro, Ray George, and Marshall Duffield.

Jones was undefeated in five Rose Bowl appearances. The first, in 1930, was noteworthy because the well-known Jock Sutherland brought in an undefeated Pitt team that got itself thrashed 47-14 as Harry Edelson, Garrett Arbelbide, Duffield, and Erny Pinckert starred and Saunders threw three touchdown passes. In 1932 USC beat undefeated Tulane 21-12. "USC has more power than any team I have ever seen," marveled Green Wave coach Bernie Bierman. In 1933 Pitt again was bashed, this time 35-0.

USC stumbled around for four years in the mid-thirties (4-6-1 in 1934, 5-7 in 1935, 4-2-3 in 1936, and 4-4-2 in 1937) and, surprisingly as it may seem of such a revered figure, Jones heard cries for his scalp. But he jazzed up his offense and came back to coach two more Rose Bowl victories.

The 1939 win over Duke was one of the most exciting in USC history. Doyle Nave, a little-used sub, was sent in to play quarterback in the last two minutes. Braven Dyer of the *Times*, who had been urging Jones to use Nave, was already on his way out of the stadium, hurrying back to his office to write the story and get the sports section out. His friend Gus Henderson was in the car with him when he heard the surprising climax on the radio.

This is what Dyer wrote for the next morning's paper:

"With the ball 34 yards from the promised land and Duke leading, 3-0, Doyle threw four consecutive strikes to Al Krueger and the last was a perfect pitch in the end zone for the winning touchdown." USC won 7-3.

Nave had not played enough minutes to earn a letter that season, but the Trojan coaching staff gave him one anyway.

Columnist Maxwell Stiles later learned that the appearance of Nave at the crucial moment was no flash of genius from stoneface Jones. Assistant coach Joe Wilensky was on the sideline manning the telephone, taking instructions from the brain-trust in the press box — assistant coaches Sam Barry, Bob McNeish, and Julie Bescos — and relaying them to Jones. Wilensky took it upon himself to pretend to be taking advice on the phone, then pass the word to send in Nave and have him pass to Krueger. When Nave heard that, he ran onto the field and Jones didn't stop him.

The Trojans were undefeated in 1939 and beat Tennessee in the 1940 Rose Bowl 14-0, but they slipped to 3-4-2 in the 1940 season. On July 27, 1941, Howard Harding Jones died of a heart attack.

"One Saturday morning in the summer of 1941 — we showed up at the office on Saturdays in those days — Howard dropped by and asked how about some golf the next day," recalled Al Wesson. "It was hot, and like an idiot, I said I planned to go to the beach instead. On the way

Al Krueger reaches for a touchdown pass in the 1940 Rose Bowl.

back from a swim at Santa Monica I tuned in to the radio and heard something like, 'We'll bet the Headman is up there now already talking it over with Knute Rockne.'

I realized that Howard had died and I headed immediately for his home in North Hollywood. When I barged into the kitchen where he had been found dead from a heart attack, and where he had often imbibed in orange juice on a Sunday morning while he told me what he'd like to say in his next syndicated yarn, or ask my advice on coming-up press interviews, I was suddenly overcome by the loss.

"Then I realized that I didn't just enjoy him, or respect him. I loved him."

"He brought a dignity and spotless reputation for clean play and high sportsmanship which no amount of money could ever buy," wrote Braven Dyer.

"I'd have to say that all of us hitched our wagon to a star, and Howard Jones was that star," said athletic director Hunter. "He made all of USC's later success possible."

In 1951 Jones was elected to the National Football Foundation Hall of Fame on the first ballot.

Justin (Sam) Barry, much better known for coaching basketball and baseball, took over for one season (2-6-1), then was succeeded by Newell (Jeff) Cravath, who had played center for Henderson and Jones in 1924, 1925, and 1926. He was captain and a unanimous All-Coast selection in his senior year. Cravath, orphaned early in his boyhood, grew up in Santa Ana, California, and was a nephew of Cliff (Gavvy) Cravath, a major-league outfielder for all or part of 12 seasons and the National League home run king five times.

Jeff had some marvelous players in his eight seasons — first-team All-Americas Ralph Heywood, John Ferraro, and Paul Cleary, and such fine future pros as quarterback Jim Hardy and defensive back Don Doll. He also had an advantage during World War II, because some top athletes from other schools were stationed at USC to take officer training: Eddie Saenz from Loyola, Mike Garzoni from Fresno State, Bill Gray and Ted Ossowski from Oregon State, among others. Hardy was almost *lost,* assigned by the Navy to Carroll College in Helena, Montana, but Cravath and the NROTC man at USC got that changed in a hurry.

Jim Hardy

Michigan's Bob Chappuis scores in the 1948 Rose Bowl game as the Wolverines humiliate the Trojans 49-0.

Because of wartime travel restrictions, the Tournament of Roses invited USC and Washington to the 1944 Rose Bowl. Washington had beaten March Field 27-7, and March Field had in turn trounced the Trojans 35-0, so the Huskies were the obvious New Year's Day favorite. But Hardy threw three touchdown passes, Norm Verry played what Cravath called "the greatest defensive game of guard the Bowl ever saw," and USC won 29-0. Washington had three passes intercepted and completed only five of 19.

Cravath had changed from the single-wing formation to the T to accommodate Hardy, Jim's pass-catching brother, Don, and other athletes, and it had been a wise move. Johnny Lynch, who refereed the game, said, "Southern California had the best team running from the T-formation I've seen since Boston College, coached by Frank Leahy, appeared in the Sugar Bowl in 1941."

In 1945 the Trojans were in the Rose Bowl again, this time whipping previously unbeaten Tennessee 25-0. John Ferraro blocked a punt and Jim Callanan took the loose ball in for a touchdown. Hardy, despite suffering from flu, played brilliantly again.

(Hardy was a terrific all-around athlete at

Troy. He played freshman basketball with Alex Hannum, who later played and coached for many years in the pros. He was a varsity baseball starter. He was a walk-on tailback for the frosh but was so obviously talented that he was soon given a football grant-in-aid. In 1943 and 1944 he led the team in total offense, passing, and punting. A two-way player — which you had to be in those times — he intercepted nine passes in 1944.)

(Because of post-war eligibility rules, Jim could have returned to USC for two more years of football after his Navy service, but he elected to turn pro instead, thinking a year of play-for-pay would buy a house while he was going to law school. The Washington Redskins had made him their first draft pick, then traded him to the Los Angeles Rams. Instead of becoming a lawyer, he had a good seven-year pro career with three teams: one season he was the second-leading passer in the NFL behind Tommy Thompson. He once threw six touchdown passes in a game, then the next game was *intercepted* eight times. He still holds that record. Today he is the general manager of Los Angeles Memorial Coliseum, where his dad often used to operate a teletype machine in the press box on Saturday and Sunday afternoons.)

World War II, of course, touched the lives of every coach, player, and fan, but none more so than the Callanans. Howard Callanan was a star wingback on Cravath's first team in 1942. The next season he was a Navy trainee and played only half the season. He was killed when his ship went down in the Pacific near the Philippines. Word of this death reached the unbeaten Trojans of 1944 on the eve of their second game that season versus Cal.

"He was the finest boy I ever coached," said Cravath after the game. "I have never known a finer family than the Callanans. We've had three of them on our squad and all any of them ever said to me was 'Yes, sir,' or 'No, sir,' or 'I'll try, sir.' His brother George wanted to play the whole game for Howard Saturday and cried when I finally took him out."

USC had tied Cal 6-6 earlier in the year but won the rematch 32-0.

After the war, things did not go so well for Cravath. After eight wins in eight appearances, USC got smashed in two Rose Bowl games, 34-14 by Alabama and Harry Gilmer in 1946 and 49-0 by Michigan and Bob Chappuis in 1948. Henry (Red) Sanders was hired to coach UCLA and in his second season, 1950, the Bruins embarrassed the Trojans 39-0. Jeff's record in 1950 was 2-5-2, his only losing season, but he finished by upsetting Notre Dame 9-7.

"The players carried me off the field on their shoulders on that glorious Saturday afternoon — and on the following Tuesday I was fired," he said.

"President (Fred) Fagg said he deeply regretted having to ask me to resign, but that his 'hands were tied.' He added that the 'boys downtown' — those with the endowment-available money — had wanted it that way and had suggested the school pay me off on my contract, which still had two years and nine months to run."

Cravath moved to a cattle and produce farm near El Centro, California, and also worked for a while as a placing judge in Santa Anita. In 1953, he died in a freak accident.

Cravath's departure came at the end of a little more than 60 years of Trojan football: six decades that had seen a little Methodist school in a sunny backwater become a large, famous university in a great metropolis, six decades in which USC had

Jeff Cravath

27

Tommy Walker

established itself as a center of dentistry, music, journalism, cinema, medicine, architecture — and football. Thirty years ago at the dawn of the television age, before the coaching reigns of Jess Hill, Don Clark, John McKay, and John Robinson, USC had started its great rivalries with Notre Dame and UCLA, produced three national-championship teams and 23 first-team All-Americas, won eight of 10 Rose Bowl games and won more than 70 percent of its games overall.

Better things were in store for USC football, but Henderson, Jones, Cravath, and many others had laid down an excellent foundation. One of the best shows in town, then as now, was going out to the Coliseum to see the Trojans conquer or be conquered.

Of course, there is much more to a USC football game than just football. In front of the rooting section the Knights, a service group, keep a Trojan sword pointed in the direction they want the team to march. Yell leaders exhort the undergraduates and alumni to scream themselves hoarse. Beautiful pompon girls do smart routines to peppy music (USC didn't have pompon girls until the 1960s, lagging far behind UCLA in this category of collegiate hoopla). Halftime card stunts entertain the other side of the Coliseum with everything from cartoons to the flowing USC signature in cardinal and gold.

And there is loud, splendid music, almost the heartbeat of college football. The Trojan marching band plays *Fight On,* one of the best-known college fight songs in America (composed by Vernon Grant and a Pasadena dentist, Dr. Milo Sweet). Or it plays *Cardinal and Gold* by Al Wesson, composed originally for a school show in 1921. Wesson, later to be a sports publicist for USC and Hollywood Park race track, was still an undergraduate when he wrote USC's alma mater, *All Hail,* while transporting *Daily Trojan* page proofs in a streetcar.

The band, like the football team, has had down years. *Daily Trojan* sports writer Steve Harvey, infamous as the creator of the *Bottom Ten* football poll that is carried by newspapers all over the nation, exposed the fact that the band one season had ringers — people toting instruments and filling out the halftime formations but unable to play a note.

Probably the most famous alumnus of the band is Herb Alpert, leader of the Tijuana Brass and head of A&M Records, but no doubt the best known band member was Tommy Walker. He was both the drum major and the football team's placekicker in 1947. He would march and sit with the musicians while wearing his band uniform over his football uniform (no shoulder pads). When coach Cravath needed a point after touchdown, Walker would shed his band togs (no need to dart into a telephone booth *a la* Clark Kent) and run out onto the field to try the kick. He made 20 extra points that season.

Cravath made him stay on the field with the team for the 1948 Rose Bowl game. Michigan stomped USC that afternoon 49-0, and Walker was immensely disappointed not only by the score but by his not getting to see action in the classic. In the sad, waning moments, Cravath ordered him to get in as a defensive back, just so he could say he played in the game, but he had to get on shoulder pads first. He was still putting them on when the gun sounded. Walker, a school of music graduate, later participated in three Super Bowls and 14 Pro Bowls — as entertainment director.

Walker went to the Washington Redskins' training camp, but while he was there he received a summons from his alma mater. "Some folks from SC asked if I wanted to become director of the band. After seeing all those big guys in practice, I said I would." He was director from 1948 to 1955.

It was during his term as band director that

USC adopted *Conquest*, the stirring music composed by Alfred Newman for the 1947 Tyrone Power movie *Captain From Castile*. And with the music, the Trojan warrior astride the white horse. (Since a horse was the downfall of ancient Troy, it's obvious Walker didn't consult the history department about his idea.) The first rider was Arthur J. Gontier III, a member of the Trojan Knights, and the first horse was rented.

"I was tall and skinny," Gontier said, "and I could hardly keep the horse on the track. We were laughed at all the way around the track."

The first regular horse was Rockazor (or Rocky), a five-gaited gelding, and the first regular rider was Bob Caswell, Architecture '42, a rancher and photo shop owner who had seen Gontier's struggle and offered the services of himself and his steed.

The band would play *Conquest* and out from the Coliseum tunnel would burst Rockazor and Caswell, who wore a flowing cardinal cape, cardinal-plumed helmet, shin guards and sandals, and carried a sword and shield. The helmet was a World War I German helmet cut up and reassembled; the plume was made of paint-brush bristles.

Caswell was succeeded by Richard Saukko, who first wore a leather outfit he made himself and later changed to a costume from the movie *Ben-Hur.* Rockazor was succeeded by Traveler I, an experienced movie horse, and then by Traveler II (a Tennessee walking horse named Little Society Gent when the university bought him at a ranch in Hidden Hills).

UCLA has never tried to kidnap the Trojan horse, but Saukko takes precautions anyway. Traveler is moved to a secret location prior to the big game every year.

"The biggest thing I worry about is Traveler getting hit by some object thrown from the stands," said Saukko. "I use the shield to ward off the debris . . ."

While the horse is perfect for spectacle, the greatest mascot USC ever had was a mutt, a mongrel, an irascible stray pooch: George Tirebiter, described once by a *Los Angeles Times* reporter as "somewhat shabby, somewhat brown, somewhat airdale." The late Jeannette Bruce, a USC alumna, wrote a fond reminiscence of Tirebiter for *Sports Illustrated* and recalled that the dog had had "the personality of a storm trooper."

Tirebiter became a campus character in the early 1940s, chasing cars and snapping at tires up and down University Avenue, which runs by Doheny Library, the Student Union, and the Tommy Trojan statue (it has been closed to traffic now for more than 20 years). Eventually George became the official Trojan mascot and was taken to the football games — often, in fact, in a limosine right behind the limo of white-maned university president Rufus B. von KleinSmid. As the limos circled the Coliseum running track, von KleinSmid waved to acknowledge the cheers which were really meant mostly for Tirebiter, who became even more of a hero when he bit Oskie, a Cal student wearing a bear head.

In 1947 some UCLA students kidnapped him from an animal hospital on West Slauson Avenue, causing a hullabaloo in the newspapers. When he was finally returned he had "UCLA" neatly and conspicuously sheared in his fur. Some sorority women knitted him a sweater so he could appear at the 1948 Rose Bowl game without advertising the crosstown rival.

In 1950 Tirebiter was retired to an animal shelter in El Centro. In September of that year he met a fitting end — run over by an automobile. The *Daily Trojan* used a second-coming-of-the-messiah headline to announce, "TIREBITER IS DEAD!" The Trojan marching band led a funeral procession on University Avenue and a cardinal and gold wreath was placed around his pawprints, preserved in cement beside various footprints of Trojan All-Americas. Various replacements and bogus descendants were tried, but none had Tirebiter's charisma or bite.

Tirebiter has a transcript on file at the school, showing he earned a 3.2 grade average in such courses as Chasing Cats 101, Biting Tires 270, and Biting People 290.

Pla

yers

It used to be that to play end or back for USC —
with few exceptions — a man had to have an
aristocratic name. The Harry Smiths, Ernie
Smiths, Johnny Bakers, and Ray Georges could
play in the line, but for the glamour positions it
had to be names from the stag line of a debu-
tante's coming-out party: Ambrose Schindler,
Orville Mohler, Irvine Eugene Warburton, Morley Drury, Elwyn Caley, Homer Griffith, Grenville Lansdell, Gaius Shaver, Marshall Duffield,
Morton Kaer, Garrett Arbelbide, and Francis
Tappaan. And let us not ignore Marger Apsit,
who, despite having a name that sounded like a
Latin grammatical term, was tough enough to
play three years in the pros.

USC has produced 69 first-team All-Americas
— Kaer, Drury, Tappaan, Arbelbide, Mohler,
Shaver, Warburton, and Lansdell among them —
but most, and dozens of less-recognized stars,
have had their days in the Coliseum sun and been
forgotten. Extraordinary athletes are now lines of
small type in a press guide. Cheers and yardage
and bruises are now confined to a file folder in the
sports information director's office, or the fading
memories of old men.

Orv Mohler from Alhambra, California, was the
son of a Pacific Coast League baseball star. If he
is remembered at all, it's as the man who held the
ball for Johnny Baker's field goal that upset Notre
Dame in 1931. But he was much more than that.
A 165-pound quarterback in Howard Jones's
single-wing attack, he gained 172 yards against
UCLA in his first varsity game (1930). He scored
four touchdowns against Cal the same year (including 78- and 64-yard runs). In 1931 he and
Gaius Shaver were neck and neck for the conference scoring title. Near the Georgia goal in the
last game, Mohler called Shaver's signal, Gaius
scored and won the title. In 1932 Mohler hit .500
to lead the California Intercollegiate Baseball Association. He gained 2,025 yards in his football
career, despite missing part of his senior year with
an injury. He was student body president.

After forays into pro baseball and the oil business, Mohler became a career Air Force officer
during World War II. He died in a plane crash in
Alabama in 1949. USC retired his number, 24,
but somebody forgot or chose to ignore it —
Anthony Gibson and Calvin Sweeney have worn
the number recently.

Mort Kaer from Red Bluff, California, in the

Jim Sears runs against Northwestern in 1952.

north Sacramento Valley, became USC's first
All-America back, in 1926. He ran and passed for
41 touchdowns and still, 55 years later, ranks in
the top 20 of Trojan rushing leaders. Oh, Morton
Armor Kaer could run and compete all right: he
won the 400-meter hurdles in the U.S. Olympic
Trials by throwing himself flat on his face at the
finish. At the 1924 Olympics in Paris, the Trojan
sophomore was third in the pentathlon (long
jump, javelin, 200-meter dash, discus, and
1,500-meter run). Later he coached two decades
of winning high school teams in tiny Weed, California, near his home town of Red Bluff.

Marshall Duffield of Santa Monica was a Howard Jones quarterback in 1928, 1929, and 1930,
when the Thundering Herd built a 27-4-1 record.
Sports writer Maxwell Stiles, then of the *Los
Angeles Examiner,* nicknamed him "Field Marshall" Duffield. He won the Trojan Diamond
Medal for "notable athletic ability, excellent
scholastic achievement, and the highest type of
sportsmanship." He was also nominated for a
Rhodes Scholarship, but the examination was on
the same day as the final game of the 1930 season,
and Duffield chose football. (What a shame.
Notre Dame hammered USC that day 27-0.)

Duffield commanded a minesweeper in World
War II and survived the invasion of Okinawa,
then returned to civilian life and became a

wealthy businessman.

Ernie Smith of Gardena, California, a 218-pound tackle of the early 1930s, was an outstanding lineman on two national-championship teams — blocking, tackling, kicking off, and placekicking (with shoes the size of kayaks). Curly Lambeau, his coach on the Green Bay Packers, called him "without question one of the best tackles ever known — truly an all-time college and pro player."

Smith played on two Rose Bowl winners and fondly recalled the first:

"In 1932, we beat Tulane 21 to 12. All-American end Jerry Dalrymple said that he would stand on a one-legged milking stool and stop the Erny Pinckert reverse, where both the right guard and right tackle pull out and lead the play. Erny Pinckert scored the second time that we used that particular play."

Jim Sears of Inglewood, California, an All-America defensive back as well as a fine runner, was overshadowed because he was squeezed in between the eras of Frank Gifford and Jon Arnett. He was an exciting punt and kickoff returner and led the Trojans in passing, scoring, and total offense in 1952. In 1950 he ran a kickoff back 44 yards for a touchdown to help beat Notre Dame 9-7. In 1952 he returned a punt 69 yards against Cal and had a hand in both touchdowns in the 14-12 victory over UCLA.

"It's kind of funny," he said. "I came to USC as an offensive back and became an All-America defensive back. Frank Gifford . . . began as a defensive back and ended up as an All-America offensive back."

Jess Hill, upon his retirement from USC, was asked to name his favorite Trojan athlete:

"Impossible, there have been so many. But Jim Sears maybe comes closest. He weighed only 160 going both ways . . . He was the most dedicated player I've ever seen."

Only Notre Dame and perhaps Michigan have had as many outstanding players over so long a time. And the talent recruited and developed by USC coaches in the last two decades has been incredible. Plums have been picked from high school backfields and lines all over the country, but most have come from California, a state rich in such natural resources as tailbacks and tackles.

USC produces dentists, medical doctors, architects, pharmacists, actors, musicians, film makers, journalists, teachers, and lawyers by the thousands, but it is also the number-one supplier of prime beef and brains to the National Football League. In 1979 there were 37 ex-Trojans on NFL rosters (Oklahoma was second with 31, Colorado third with 29). In 1980 the NFL had 45 ex-Trojans playing (plus alumnus Monte Clark coaching the Detroit Lions and former head coach, John McKay, coaching the Tampa Bay Buccaneers), compared to 36 from Penn State and 35 from Oklahoma.

More than 240 Trojan football players have performed in professional leagues. Alphabetically they range from guard Pete Adams of Cleveland to tight end Charles Young of Philadelphia, Los Angeles, and San Francisco. Chronologically: from end John Milton in 1923 to the present rookie crop. And geographically: from end Bill Fisk of the Hollywood Bears and Los Angeles Dons to safety Sandy Durko of New England (plus Jimmy Jones, Elmer Willhoite, and others who played in the Canadian Football League). Second-string Trojans have made the pros, e.g. running back Allen Carter of New England. Non-*lettermen* have made the pros, e.g. Dick Dorsey of the 1962 Oakland Raiders.

Three ex-Trojans, end Morris (Red) Badgro and back Frank Gifford, both of the New York Giants, and tackle Ron Mix of San Diego and Oakland, have been elected to the Pro Football Hall of Fame in Canton, Ohio. Buffalo running back O.J. Simpson and Green Bay safety Willie Wood are sure to follow. Fifteen alumni have made first-team All-Pro in the AFL or NFL, 33 were first-round draft picks.

And talk about high honors!: back Homer Griffith of the Chicago Cardinals and tackle Ernie Smith of Green Bay were included in the rare 1935 National Chicle bubble-gum card set, the first nationally distributed set devoted exclusively to football players and coaches. A mint-condition Smith card is worth about $10, a mint-condition Griffith about $3.50.

What follows is a gallery of USC football greats, presented in somewhat larger-than-bubble-gum-card form. It is a lineup — Arnett, Drury, Simpson, Garrett, McDonald, Bell, White — that should shake down the thunder and wake up the echoes for anybody who has ever seen a Trojan team burst out of the Coliseum tunnel at full speed as the band strikes up *Fight On*.

Morley Drury

Jess Hill

Erny Pinckert

Morley Drury
Quarterback 1925, 26, 27

"I was listening to a USC-Washington game on radio as a kid in 1927," said Nick Pappas, now an associate athletic director at USC. "It was Morley Drury's final game and they gave him a standing ovation for 10 minutes at the Coliseum. Right then I knew I wanted to play for USC and Howard Jones." Drury played quarterback for Jones (roughly similar to tailback today) and "back back" (safety) on defense. In that game Pappas listened to, the Canadian-born Drury gained 180 yards and scored three touchdowns. He was 6-0, 185-pounds, the second-biggest man on the team, and was older than his teammates, having entered USC at 21. Versatile and durable, he once carried the ball 41 times versus Cal, and he also lettered in water polo, ice hockey, and basketball. "He was a great leader," said center Nate Barragar. "He was superb under pressure."

Jess Hill
Fullback 1928, 29

Howard Jones had such stockpiles of talent in 1928 and 1929 that the two most versatile athletes in USC history, Jess Mortensen and Jess Hill, were only subs. Fullback Hill had his moments, though, such as the afternoon he got in a game in Seattle and gained more than 150 yards. Unfortunately, the radio announcer called him Cliff Thiede throughout the contest, and Thiede hadn't even made the trip. Hill, a barber's son from Corona in Riverside County, was also a *cum laude* student in pre-med, the first Trojan to long jump 25 feet (in 1929), and an outstanding outfielder (he played three years in the American League, batting .289). He coached track at USC for three years (two NCAA titles), football for six (.722 winning percentage), and was athletic director for 15, during which USC won 31 national titles.

Erny Pinckert
Halfback 1929, 30, 31

Erny Pinckert, like Drury a member of the National Football Hall of Fame, was a fine runner — proven by his 30- and 27-yard touchdown runs (on reverses) in the 1932 Rose Bowl victory over Tulane. But Howard Jones used him principally as a blocker for the likes of Russ Saunders, Marshall Duffield, Gaius Shaver, and Orv Mohler, and Pinckert didn't seem to mind: "I got a great deal of satisfaction out of knocking down those big tackles." He could also draw cartoons, catch footballs (Saunders hit him with a touchdown pass in the 1930 Rose Bowl), and play defense (he caught a Tulane halfback from behind after a 59-yard gain, preventing a touchdown). USC's second two-time All-America played nine years for the Washington Redskins, then built a successful clothes-designing business. He died in 1977 at his West Los Angeles home, which he had designed himself.

Irvine (Cotton) Warburton

Aaron Rosenberg

Irvine (Cotton) Warburton

Quarterback 1932, 33, 34

"He rates as the best small back in college history," said Paul Schwegler, Washington State lineman of the 1930s. "He was lightning, tough as hell, and hard to believe," said teammate Aaron Rosenberg. The subject: Irvine Eugene (Cotton) Warburton, the 5-6½, 145-pound quarterback who starred for the Howard Jones teams of 1932, 1933, and 1934. As a 132-pound sophomore he was Troy's leading rusher in the 13-0 win over Notre Dame, and he scored two fourth-quarter touchdowns in the Rose Bowl. As a junior he scored twice against the Irish and set up a third touchdown, prompting Grantland Rice to write, "The Cottontop is marvelous and incredible and he sent the home club into a tailspin. Notre Dame stopped all the Trojans but this one . . ."

Warburton played defense, too. In the 6-3 win over Cal in 1933, he tackled brawny Harry Jones in the open field to prevent a touchdown and had to be carried off the field. In the second half he went 60 yards for the winning touchdown. He couldn't remember anything about the play afterward.

Cotton became a film editor, and in 1965 he won an Oscar for editing *Mary Poppins*. He retired in 1979.

Aaron Rosenberg

Guard 1931, 32, 33

USC was 30-2-1 in Aaron Rosenberg's three years as a guard and linebacker and he reaped much of the credit (All-America two years, National Football Hall of Fame, All-Time Rose Bowl team picked in 1971, etc.). Quarterback Cotton Warburton, who followed Rosie's blocks for two seasons, said the journalism major was one of the fastest men on the team. "And not just fast but tough. He played with broken cheekbones, sprains, and just about anything else. When he'd knock guys down, they'd stay down." Instead of journalism or pro football, Rosenberg chose motion pictures after graduation, starting as a $40-a-week second-assistant director at 20th Century-Fox. Eventually he produced 70 movies including *Mutiny on the Bounty* (Marlon Brando version), *The Glenn Miller Story*, and *Winchester 73*. He died in 1979.

John Ferraro

John Ferraro

Tackle 1943, 44, 46, 47

As if he didn't have enough advantage being 6-4 and 240 to 260 pounds (depending on which listing you believe), tackle John Ferraro got to play four years of varsity football at USC; World War II changed the eligibility rules. (This was before freshmen could play varsity.) Ferraro's teammate and fraternity brother, quarterback Jim Hardy, could have played a fourth year also but elected to turn pro. Jeff Cravath considered Ferraro the second best tackle in USC history, behind Ray George and ahead of Ernie Smith and Jesse Hibbs. After his game against San Diego Navy in 1944, the *Los Angeles Times'* Braven Dyer wrote, "If any tackle in this land of ours has ever played better ball, he must be Superman and Hercules rolled into one. When Big John goes to work, he's dynamite." Today Ferraro is a Los Angeles city councilman and potential mayor.

Frank Gifford

Tailback 1949, 50, 51

Frank Gifford, the solid citizen of ABC's Monday-night television football and Dry Sack commercials, was once a constant truant as a Bakersfield high-school kid. The chance to play football at USC got him working harder on the books, but he still had to go to junior college first (as O.J. Simpson and others did later). Gifford didn't become a star until his senior year in 1951, when Jess Hill became head coach and made him a single-wing tailback; he had played mostly defense and placekicker before. He led USC's celebrated 1951 upset of Cal at Berkeley, leading a magazine to write, "His slashing runs and clutch passes spearheaded the three-touchdown rally which ended California's recent domination of West Coast football." Army coach Red Blaik praised him highly after he gained 138 muddy yards in Yankee Stadium against the Cadets. Frank was a star for the New York Giants for 12 seasons and was inducted into the Pro Football Hall of Fame, in Canton, Ohio, in 1977.

Frank Gifford

Elmer Willhoite (73) and Marv Goux (20)

Jon Arnett

Halfback 1954, 55, 56

There are some Trojan fans who will agree that the greatest USC runner, post-World War II, was not Simpson, Davis, White, Bell, or Garrett, but Jon Arnett, two-way star of the mid-1950s. Jaguar Jon, a fine tumbler and long jumper at Manual Arts High, was fast, tough, and had extraordinary balance. "I thought Jon Arnett was fantastic," Mike Garrett once told the *Los Angeles Times*. "I think he is one of the greatest runners who ever lived." A few of his feats: 28 points against Oregon, including a 90-yard punt return; a 97-yard kickoff return versus UCLA, nullified by penalty, and 128 yards in the mud against Ohio State in the 1955 Rose Bowl. He also punted, kicked extra points, passed well, and played superbly on defense. Because of conference penalties, he played only five games his senior year, or he, not Garrett, might have been USC's first Heisman Trophy winner.

Elmer Willhoite

Guard 1951, 52

Televised football was fairly new in 1952, but already USC was providing thrills for armchair fans. The big play in the Trojans' 14-12 victory over UCLA that season was Elmer Ellsworth Willhoite intercepting Paul Cameron's pass in the third quarter and taking it 72 yards to the Bruin eight. Guard Willhoite, a tough Dutch kid from Merced who also put the shot and threw the discus, made both the offensive and defensive all-league teams that year, and *Look Magazine's* All-America. Perhaps his tendency to fisticuffs was shown in the 1953 Rose Bowl game against Wisconsin: he was thrown out in the fourth quarter for unnecessary roughness. He played some Canadian professional football and was an amateur boxer for 18 months (unbeaten in eight bouts) before brittle hands forced him to hang up the gloves.

Marv Goux

Center and Linebacker 1952, 54, 55

It was the night before a USC-Notre Dame game at South Bend. Trojan assistant coach Marv Goux stood up in front of a Fighting Irish support group and led it in singing the Notre Dame fight song; he knew the words as well as anybody in the hall. "Know thy enemy," he told the audience. Goux loves the USC-Notre Dame game ("You can smell blood in the air"). Goux loves football — particularly USC football. He was a 5-10, 185-pound center and linebacker in the mid-1950s and twice won the Davis-Teschke Award as the most inspirational member of the team. He joined Don Clark as an assistant in 1957 and has stayed on through the regimes of John McKay and John Robinson, recruiting players like O.J. Simpson and coaching more All-America linemen than most schools have had in their entire histories.

Jon Arnett

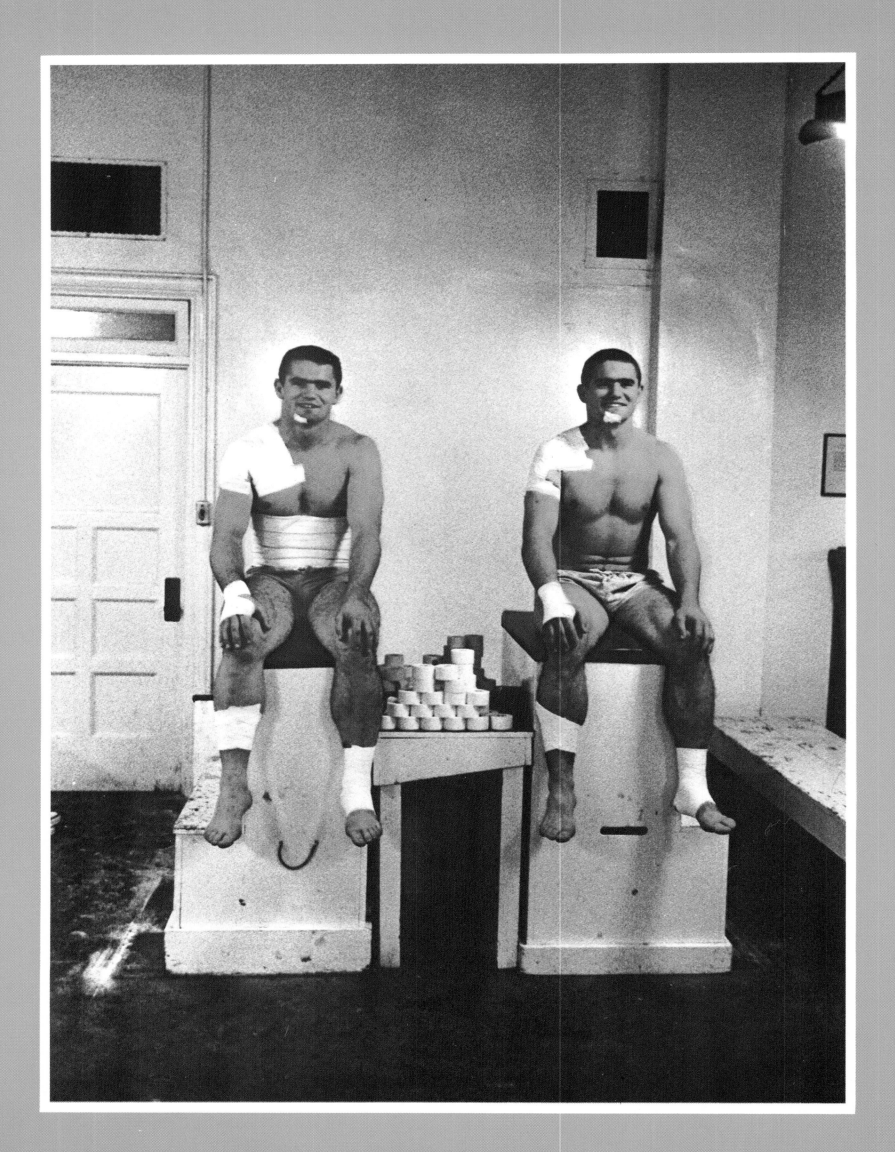

Marlin and Mike McKeever

Ron Mix (74) and Willie Wood (16)

Marlin McKeever

End and Fullback 1958, 59, 60

Mike McKeever

Guard and Linebacker 1958, 59, 60

Marlin and Mike McKeever, each 6-1, 230 to 240 pounds, were perhaps the greatest twin athletes of all time. All-America Mike, a linebacker and guard, led the entire Trojan team in defensive statistics as a sophomore and junior and probably would have led a third time except that a head injury put him out of football for good. All-America Marlin, who played end and some fullback, was named Associated Press lineman of the week as a senior for his play against Georgia. As juniors they were co-AP linemen of the week for double-handedly battering Baylor. They were also valuable weight men for the track team.

Controversy and tragedy struck Mike from 1959 on. When he was a junior, he landed on Cal's Steve Bates out of bounds and severely injured the Bear's halfback. Cal complained bitterly about the incident, and USC president Norman Topping apologized. As a senior Mike had to have surgery to remove blood clots from his brain, ruining his and Marlin's plans to play pro football together. On December 3, 1965 he suffered a serious head injury, this time in an automobile accident. He lapsed into a coma and never recovered, dying in August, 1967. Marlin went on to a successful NFL career with Los Angeles, Minnesota, Philadelphia, and Washington, playing linebacker and tight end.

Willie Wood

Quarterback and Defensive Back 1957, 58, 59

Willie Wood earned most of his football fame as a six-time All-Pro defensive back for the great Green Bay Packer teams coached by Vince Lombardi. But the Washington, D.C. product also has a special niche at USC, where he passed, ran, and defended with skill in the late 1950s. He had to share quarterbacking duties with Tom Maudlin as a sophomore and with Ben Charles as a senior (a shoulder injury curtailed his play in his junior year), but he had few peers in the defensive backfield. He led USC's defensive-secondary statistics as a sophomore and was a close second as a senior. People who saw him play in person or on television will most likely remember the thrilling, last-minute Trojan comebacks he led with his long passes. He once had a 75-yard punt return.

Ron Mix

End and Tackle 1957, 58, 59

As a senior at Hawthorne High, Ron Mix was merely an honorable mention all-league end. He played end for the frosh at USC and stayed at that position as a sophomore. As a junior he was moved to tackle but had to play behind Monte Clark (later a fine pro). Finally, as a senior, playing in a line that also had the McKeever twins and Dan Ficca, Mix made one All-America team (NBC's) as a tackle and was first-team All-Coast and all-conference. The improvement didn't stop there by any means. Mix became one of the greatest offensive linemen in professional history with the San Diego Chargers and was elected to the Pro Football Hall of Fame in 1979.

43

Hal Bedsole

Hal Bedsole

End 1961, 62, 63

Moving 6-5 Hal Bedsole to receiver was one of the most inspired position switches in USC history. He entered school as a quarterback but found Pete Beathard and Bill Nelsen ahead of him. He had *never* caught a pass in a game, yet as a sophomore he became Helms Athlete of the Month for October, 1961. He was even better as a junior (33 catches for 827 yards and 11 TDs) and had two touchdown receptions against Wisconsin in the 1963 Rose Bowl. The cocky Bedsole got temporary butterfingers as a senior and was once demoted to third string, but by season's end pro scouts were drooling again. A consensus All-America, he was selected by the Minnesota Vikings in the 1964 NFL draft, where he was made a tight end.

Athletic director Jess Hill loved Prince Hal: ". . . Bedsole has size, speed, strength, a fine pair of hands, and he can do more with a football after he catches it than any end I have ever seen, and that includes the pros."

Willie Brown

Halfback 1961, 62, 63

Willie Brown, a fine runner, receiver, and defensive back (and not a bad baseball player either), was one of the most heralded high school stars USC ever recruited. He had averaged 13.5 yards a carry as a senior at Long Beach Poly, alma mater of Morley Drury. A three-year starting halfback for McKay's finest early teams, Brown first broke loose against SMU as a junior, taking the opening kickoff 92 yards for a touchdown. Other notable 1962 exploits: an average of 17.88 yards per carry versus Navy, a 5.25 average against Notre Dame, and three catches for 108 yards in the 1963 Rose Bowl victory over Wisconsin. On defense in that game he made a vital interception. As a senior he set a good example for newcomer Mike Garrett with such performances as two touchdown catches against Stanford and a 49-yard scoring run versus Ohio State.

Willie Brown

45

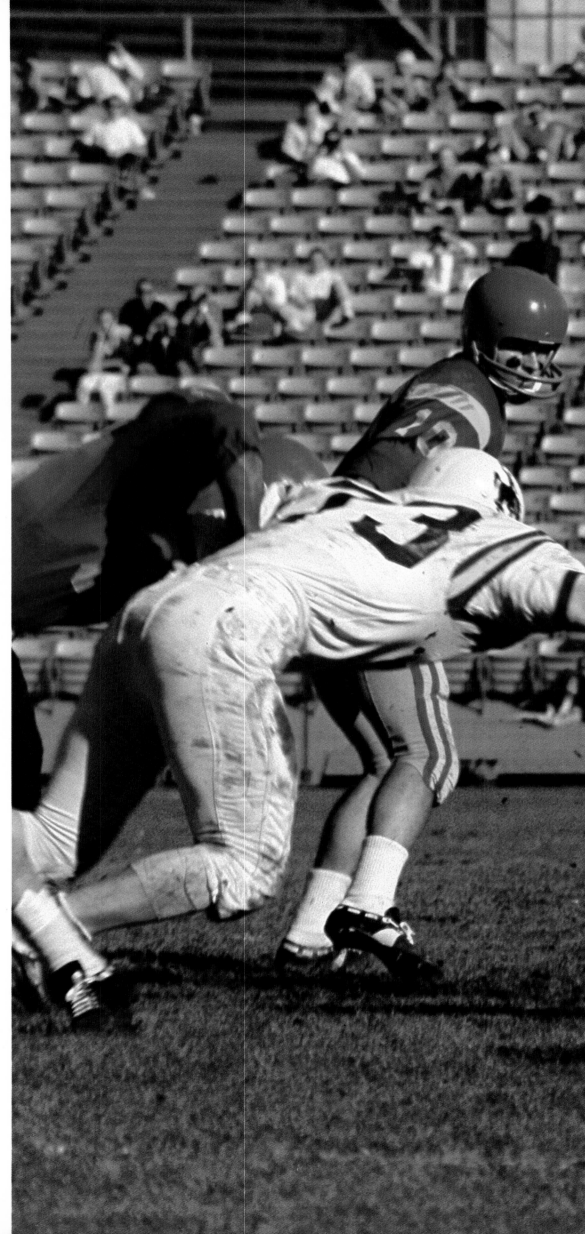

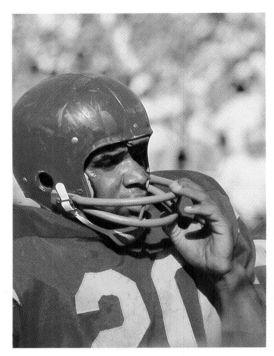

Mike Garrett

Tailback 1963, 64, 65

Mike Garrett—"The Duck" to his teammates and "Iron Mike" to the media— was a quick-cutting broken-field runner in the manner of Jon Arnett. A stubby 5-9, 180-185 pounds, he was USC's first Heisman Trophy winner, set an NCAA career rushing record (3,221 yards), and was called by John McKay ". . . not only the greatest player I have coached, but the greatest college player I have ever seen."

Garrett, like Arnett before him and Clarence Davis, Anthony Davis, Ricky Bell, and Charles White after, came out of the Los Angeles City Schools. He was excellent as a sophomore (seventh in the nation in rushing), superb as a junior, and absolutely the best in the country as a senior in 1965: Garrett had touchdown punt returns of 74 and 87 yards versus Cal, and three touchdowns apiece against Oregon State, Pitt, and Wyoming. Only Notre Dame was able to stop him (43 yards net).

Garrett was the first of McKay's great I-formation tailbacks, able to dart to daylight, then burrow, squirm, and dance his way to the goal line. It was Garrett who started the tailback tradition of dashing 40 yards or so on every run in practice.

Despite his excellence, Garrett never played in a Rose Bowl game. In his first season as a professional, he played for Kansas City in Super Bowl I and, three years later, starred in the Chiefs' Super Bowl IV victory over the Minnesota Vikings.

Adrian Young

Adrian Young

Linebacker 1965, 66, 67

How ironic that when USC beat the Fighting Irish at South Bend in 1967—its first win there in 28 years—the man calling defensive signals for the Trojans was handsome Matthew Adrian Young, an Irishman born in Dublin (of course, Irish linebackers weren't entirely new at Troy, Irishman John McKay having coached both Mike McKeever and Damon Bame). Young spent part of his youth in Ireland, then the family moved to California. Because of maturation and exhausting weight work, he grew from a 153-pound cornerback as a sophomore at Bishop Amat High to the 224-pound defensive captain of USC's 11-1, national-championship team of 1967. Young was a consensus All-America and later a fine professional, playing for the Philadelphia Eagles.

Rod Sherman

Flanker 1964, 65, 66

Redhead Rod Sherman was a star on the 1962 UCLA freshman team but transferred to USC (via Pasadena JC) because he thought John McKay would make him a better quarterback. Instead, McKay made him a pass-catching halfback with a knack for clutch plays. As with the switch of Hal Bedsole, Troy got good results from Sherman right away. The 190-pound sophomore speedster caught a last-minute touchdown pass from Craig Fertig to beat Cal in 1964 and had another clutch touchdown reception to beat undefeated Notre Dame. Sherman, who had been a champion hurdler at Pasadena's Muir High, was also a good runner: as a junior he averaged eight yards a carry versus Cal and had a 44-yard touchdown run against Wisconsin. As a senior he had a spectacular 76-yard touchdown run against Oregon State. He played seven years in the NFL, five of them with Oakland.

Rod Sherman

Mike Battle (17) and Tim Rossovich (88)

Tim Rossovich
Defensive End 1965, 66, 67
Mike Battle
Defensive Back 1966, 67, 68

Tim Rossovich, one-quarter Yugoslavian and three-quarters Italian, became well known as a pro for being four-quarters crazy (or at least eccentric). The press gleefully told the world of his setting himself on fire, eating glass, and playing Christmas carols all year. At USC he was an outstanding defensive end on the 1967 national-championship team that gave up only 87 points. The 6-5, 235-pound All-America was once described by John McKay as "a big boy, an intelligent boy, and above all, a mean boy."

Tall (6-1) and skinnier than a yard marker, Mike Battle nevertheless lived up to his surname and to his uncle, Art Battle, a Trojan player of the late 1940s. An ex-high school rollout quarterback, Mike was a starting defensive back for three years and a gutsy punt returner. Perhaps his finest game was against Washington State as a junior in 1967: key tackles, an interception that set up a touchdown, and a 32-yard punt return for a touchdown. Not bad for a man who probably never weighed more than 175 pounds, even in full Battle gear.

Ron Yary
Tackle 1965, 66, 67

Along with Ron Mix and Brad Budde, Ron Yary is probably one of the three greatest offensive linemen ever turned out by USC. Yary was a fullback his senior year at Bellflower High and an All-Coast defensive tackle as a Trojan sophomore, but it was as an offensive tackle, blocking for O.J. Simpson, that he won the Outland Trophy in 1967 (considered the Heisman Trophy for linemen). His weight got up as high as 270-275 as a junior, but he cut down to 255 pounds as a senior and he has kept it there most of the time as a standout professional for the Minnesota Vikings.

Ron Yary

O.J. Simpson
Tailback 1967, 68

Here is a good question to throw out the next time you are in a trivia contest: what high school turned out three athletes who would at least be candidates for the all-time greatest in baseball, basketball, and football? The answer is Galileo High in San Francisco, which produced Joe DiMaggio, Angelo (Hank) Luisetti, and O.J. Simpson. USC had Orenthal James Simpson for only two years, but what an incredible two years they were.

Simpson was one of the fastest running backs ever (despite his size: 6-2, 207). He ran a 9.4 100 and a 21.5 220 for the Trojan track team and was a member of the 1967 world-record-setting sprint relay team with Lennox Miller, Fred Kuller, and fellow footballer Earl McCullouch. When O.J. zoomed through the line, he was like a heat-seeking missile—and the heat was the goal line. At City College of San Francisco he scored 54 touchdowns in two seasons and averaged 9.3 yards a carry; at USC he was almost as spectacular. His most famous run was 64 yards to a touchdown to beat UCLA in 1967, but there were many other marvelous moments and games. Against Minnesota in the first game of his senior year, he gained 236 yards for a 6.05 average, scored four touchdowns, caught six passes for 57 yards, and returned three kickoffs for 72 yards. Long-time Georgia Tech coach Bobby Dodd and many others called Simpson the greatest player they had ever seen.

John McKay paid tribute to O.J.'s durability with wisecracks: "Only 40 carries for O.J.? Heck, he can go out dancing tonight." Or: "Simpson gets faster in the fourth quarter and I get smarter." The nation's press paid tribute in 1968 by voting him the Heisman Trophy.

Jimmy Jones

Sam Cunningham

Sam Cunningham
Fullback 1970, 71, 72

Sam Cunningham, a sprinter who had won the state shot put championship while at Santa Barbara High, spent most of his Trojan career blocking for Clarence Davis and Anthony Davis ("He's the best running back I ever ruined," joked John McKay). And quite a blocker he was. John Robinson was in his first year as a McKay aide in Sam's senior year (1972) and called the 230-pound fullback "the least-selfish man I know" and "the best blocking back I've ever seen." But Cunningham carried the ball a few times, too. He scored four times on dives over the line against Ohio State in the 1973 Rose Bowl. In his first varsity game, at Alabama, he gained 135 yards on 12 carries and scored two touchdowns. Probably USC's all-time greatest rushing fullback, he averaged 4.6 yards a carry in three seasons.

Jimmy Jones
Quarterback 1969, 70, 71

Jimmy Jones threw 30 touchdown passes for USC, but the two most important came at the end of his sophomore season, 1969. His 32-yard touchdown pass play with Sam Dickerson beat UCLA 14-12, and his 33-yard touchdown pass play to Bob Chandler helped upset Michigan in the 1970 Rose Bowl. Heavily recruited by Ohio State, Penn State, and others out of Harrisburg, Pennsylvania, Jones chose USC and was named MVP as a sophomore, was equally good as a junior, then had to share some time with talented Mike Rae as a senior. Perhaps his greatest performance came against Oregon State in 1970: 15 of 21 passes for 304 yards in a 45-13 romp. USC was 22-8-2 under his quarterbacking and 2-0-1 versus Notre Dame. The NFL wanted to make a receiver out of him, so he went to Canada and became a star there.

Lynn Swann
Flanker 1971, 72, 73

Lynn Swann had every attribute a receiver needs: determination, hands (he was a fine high-school quarterback and basketball player), speed (9.8 in the 100), leaping ability (he was the California long-jump champion in high school, beating future Olympic Gold Medalist Randy Williams). "Of all the things we ask players to do on the field," said John McKay, "Swann can do more than anybody. And he's asked to do more than anybody." One of the things he did in 1971, 1972, and 1973 was return punts: 92 yards against Michigan State, 76 versus Arkansas (nullified by a penalty), 48 against Georgia Tech. He made 95 catches for 1,562 yards in his Trojan career and, despite weighing only 179 pounds, was an effective blocker. Swann became an All-Pro wide receiver for the great Pittsburgh Steelers teams of the 1970s, and was a spectacular star of Super Bowl X.

Richard Wood
Linebacker 1972, 73, 74

No Trojan ever had a more impressive debut than linebacker Richard Wood, whose first varsity game was against the Arkansas Razorbacks in Little Rock in 1972. He was in on 18 tackles that night, harassed quarterback Joe Ferguson, and intercepted a pass. Wrote Joe Jares in *Sports Illustrated*, ". . . it was the quick, hard-tackling Wood who had the biggest part in butchering the Hogs. He is the younger brother of ex-Detroit Tiger infielder Jake Wood, and McKay says he is 'the best linebacker prospect we've had since I've been here.' A few more assault and batteries like Saturday night's and there will be nothing prospective about it." There were more than a few other games like it, and Wood, from Elizabeth, New Jersey, became the first three-year All-America at USC.

Richard Wood

Lynn Swann

Anthony Davis
Tailback 1972, 73, 74

After Anthony Davis zoomed over the 1,000-yard rushing mark for the third straight season in 1974, he took the offensive line out to dinner. That was appreciated but unnecessary, said one of the blockers, Bill Bain: "AD is a super talent. He's really doing it all by himself. When he wants to go, he goes. He doesn't need us to show him the way." He *went,* all right, even in 1973 when he had 200 pounds on his 5-9 frame (McKay made him slim down for his last season). Some highlights: six touchdowns against the Irish as a sophomore (including 97- and 96-yard kickoff returns), five touchdowns against Cal as a junior, a 102-yard kickoff return against Notre Dame as a senior (he was also a good baseball player at USC). However, all his televised explosions failed to help him wrest the Heisman Trophy from Ohio State's Archie Griffin.

Gary Jeter
Defensive Tackle 1973, 74, 75, 76

"The toughest defense I've had to run against is our own," said Ricky Bell. "Every once in a while Gary Jeter forgets and throws me down." Jeter, 6-4½, 255 pounds, was a consensus All-America defensive tackle in his fourth year as a starter, 1976. John McKay called him "the best tackle in America," and John Robinson, whose first year as head coach was Jeter's last, said, "His physical ability is awesome . . . He can absolutely dominate a game." Gary, who chose to play at USC over Notre Dame and Ohio State, was lucky to be *alive,* much less be an Adonis. He was stabbed in the chest when he was 14, the knife blade missing his heart by six inches. After that he lifted weights to build himself up and became a star at Cleveland's Cathedral Latin High. He had good genes, too: uncles Tony and Bob Jeter played at Nebraska and Iowa. In the 1976 NFL draft, Gary was selected on the first round by the New York Giants, where he has played his professional career.

Gary Jeter

Pat Haden

Quarterback 1972, 73, 74

One of the great high-school passing combinations of all time, Pat Haden to J.K. McKay, became one of USC's greatest, too. Haden, a handsome, 5-11 blond, lived with the John McKay family his senior year at Bishop Amat High (his salesman father had been transferred to San Francisco), so there wasn't much doubt which school would win the recruiting battle when he graduated. Pat played behind Mike Rae in 1972, then took over at quarterback for two years. Said coach McKay, "In all my years of football, I've never seen a passer with more accuracy than Pat Haden." He was an excellent student, too, majoring in English and earning a 3.7 grade point average out of a possible 4.0. He finished a dream college career with clutch touchdown passes against Notre Dame and Ohio State, and then won a Rhodes Scholarship to study politics, economics, and philosophy at Oxford University in England.

Marvin Powell

Tackle 1974, 75, 76

Marvin Powell, 6-5, 265 pounds, All-America tackle in 1975 and 1976 and a three-year starter, used to talk about the books he'd read rather than the defensive linemen he had flattened. An Army kid from Fayetteville, North Carolina, his father was a retired paratrooper and his stepfather had been killed in Vietnam. Powell was a William Buckley conservative and a patriot, and he was gung-ho about USC, too: ". . . standing in the Coliseum tunnel before our first game against Arkansas when they began to play *Conquest*. I can't describe the feeling, but you could have put me in a cage with King Kong right then and I would have pinned him in three seconds. It was electric." He missed four games in 1976, so he was not a consensus All-America. Powell has since become an All-Pro for the New York Jets, who selected him on the first round of the 1977 NFL draft.

Marvin Powell

Pat Haden

Ricky Bell

Fullback and Tailback 1973, 74, 75, 76

One of Ricky Bell's six brothers led a rock group, Archie Bell and the Drells. Ricky led a rock-hard group, the Trojans. In 1973 he was one of three freshmen to letter (as an outside linebacker). A fullback on the 1974 national-championship team, he cleared paths for Anthony Davis and averaged 6.6 yards a carry himself. John McKay switched him to tailback as a junior and he led the nation in rushing with the second highest total in NCAA history. UCLA's Cliff Frazier said, "Ricky Bell is the best back I've faced this year. He's fast, hard, tough, and quick, and he can run over you and around you. He's a threat every time he handles the ball." In 1976, in addition to other feats, he rushed 51 times for 346 yards against Washington State! He failed to win the Heisman Trophy but was twice voted USC's MVP. In the 1977 NFL draft, he was the first player selected, rejoining his old coach, John Mckay, in Tampa.

Brad Budde

Guard 1976, 77, 78, 79

At the end of the 1979 season, his fourth as a starting guard, Brad Budde won the Lombardi Award as the outstanding college lineman who also "exemplifies the discipline of Vince Lombardi." John Robinson raved about the 6-5, 253-pound blocker who led Charles White's interference on so many runs: "Brad is just about the ideal player. He's very tough, very intelligent, and an outstanding athlete. He's also very aggressive and very intense." Budde had good genes; his dad, Ed, had been an All-Pro guard for the Kansas City Chiefs. But it took more than genes to win him recognition as an Academic All-America and UPI's 1979 lineman of the year. "You have to love contact to play where I do," he said, "and I wouldn't trade it for anything." After signing a pro contract with Kansas City in 1980, Budde repaid USC for his grant-in-aid: $24,931.

Brad Budde

Keith Van Horne

Paul McDonald

Quarterback 1977, 78, 79

Paul McDonald was an A-student quarterback from Bishop Amat High, just like Pat Haden, but the lefty McDonald passed Haden and every other Trojan quarterback in the record book. He has the highest completion percentage, lowest interception percentage, most completions, most touchdowns, and most yardage of any USC passer. Said quarterback coach Paul Hackett, "McDonald is the engineer out there. He makes us go." For instance, the 1980 Rose Bowl versus Ohio State: 234 yards and a touchdown. Or the Arizona game in 1979: 25 completions, 380 yards, and three touchdowns. Or four touchdown passes against Cal in 1978. Despite the time taken in frequent quarterback meetings, McDonald found time to get in plenty of quiet, intense study at the Law Library. "As a leader, he's held in awe by the other players on our team," said John Robinson. "And he's flat out one of the coolest people I've ever seen."

Keith Van Horne

Tackle 1977, 78, 79, 80

Rival coaches frequently rave about USC's talent, sometimes with genuine admiration, sometimes as an excuse for losing. USC does well in the recruiting wars, no doubt, but the coaches also deserve credit for being able to spot talent. Keith Van Horne, who developed into a 1980 All-America offensive tackle and first-round draft choice by the Chicago Bears, was a good example. He was not wanted by Notre Dame or UCLA, but assistant coach Hudson Houck convinced John Robinson to take him. Van Horne added 30 or 40 pounds by lifting weights and used his 6-7 height and 265 pounds to good advantage blocking for Charlie White, Paul McDonald, and Marcus Allen. He was USC's offensive player of the year in 1980, the offensive player of the game versus UCLA, and an Academic All-America (majoring in broadcast journalism). "Among the best who have ever played here," said Robinson. Hats off to Houck.

Charles White

Tailback 1976, 77, 78, 79

Charles White was USC's second great tailback out of San Fernando High, following Anthony Davis. He was a workhorse but hardly a plodding one. In 1979 at least eight different publications and organizations named him college-football player of the year. The most important, of course, was the Downtown Athletic Club of New York, which conducted the poll that made him USC's third Heisman Trophy winner. It was no easy choice, because Oklahoma's Billy Sims was a candidate, and he had won the statuette the previous year.

White, a 5-11, 185-pound speedster (he was city, state, and national low-hurdles champ in high school and set a national record of 36.0 in the high-school 330-yard low-hurdles), piled up some amazing career stats: 5,598 regular-season yards (second highest in NCAA history), 31 times over 100 yards in a game and 22 NCAA, Pac-10, USC, and Rose Bowl records set or equaled. "He does some amazing things out there," said quarterback Paul McDonald. "He takes so much pressure off me. . ." White had a particularly fine game on national TV against Notre Dame in 1979: 44 carries for 261 yards. The following week, John Robinson said, "He's only missed two Mondays all year. If that was me, I'd say, 'Hey, baby, I carried the ball 44 times Saturday. You can bring my coffee and doughnuts to the whirlpool Monday.' "

In 1980, White became the first draft choice of the NFL's Cleveland Browns, and, ironically, was reunited with McDonald, who was selected by the Browns on the fourth round.

DANIELLE DIETRICH
Director
General Alumni Association

TO SID AND HELEN

TROJANS FOREVER

for
Sid Chambers

Alumni House
University of Southern California
Los Angeles, California 90007
(213) 743-2300

Chip Banks

Chip Banks
Linebacker 1978, 79, 80, 81

Georgia has been good to USC in the John Robinson era: Joey and Keith Browner, Walt Underwood, August Curley, and William (Chip) Banks, the master linebacker from Augusta. Banks led the Pac-10's top defensive team in tackles and tackles for a loss in 1980, and wowed viewers of game films. Coaches came out of the Notre Dame and Arizona films as if they had just seen a surefire Oscar winner. Chip made sensational interceptions in both games. Against the Irish he snatched a pass out of the air five yards from the quarterback and returned it 49 yards to the Irish 1. Against Arizona he was yanked down by a blocker, got up, leaped to deflect a pass, pivoted in the air, dived and caught the ball before it hit the turf. Before 1981 spring practice, Robinson said, "Chip can become the dominant defensive player in college football this year. . . ."

Marcus Allen
Tailback 1978, 79, 80, 81

Marcus Allen is perhaps the most versatile of the I-formation tailbacks who have played at USC. In 1978, he averaged 5.5 yards a carry as Charles White's backup. He played fullback in 1979, blocking well for White and averaging 5.7 yards himself. He was back to tailback as a junior and was second in the nation in rushing, first in all-purpose running, first on the team in receiving. Not bad for a man recruited out of San Diego's Lincoln High as a defensive back. "Marcus is one of the great players in the country—and he's still improving," said John Robinson. "He's a superb runner and an accurate passer (he played quarterback in high school, too), his blocking for the quarterback is outstanding, and he's one of the best pass-receiving backs I've ever seen in college football."

Marcus Allen

Riv

alries

Knute Rockne

USC versus Notre Dame is without question the greatest intersectional rivalry in college football. More than 25 years ago, before 10 or 12 of the most exciting and important games had been played, *Sport Magazine* called it "The Great Irish-Trojan War." The classic series began in 1926, when dour Calvin Coolidge was president of the United States and travelers rode the friendly rails instead of flying the friendly skies.

In fact, it was aboard a train from Lincoln, Nebraska, to Chicago in November of 1925 that the deal was struck for a home-and-home series. USC had just joined the Pacific Coast Conference but had no traditional rival. Washington had Washington State, Oregon had Oregon State, California had Stanford — but USC did *not* have UCLA, which was still the Southern Branch of the University of California and a member of the Southern California Intercollegiate Association. The Bruins that season lost to Stanford 82-0 and only managed a tie with Caltech 10-10.

Gwynn Wilson, later to be president of the USC Alumni Association, assistant general manager of the Los Angeles Olympic Games, and part owner of Santa Anita, was at the time USC's graduate manager (there is no such position today). Wilson approached Dr. Harold J. Stonier, USC's financial vice-president (and Wilson's Kappa Alpha fraternity brother), and suggested scheduling a football game with the Fighting Irish. Stonier took the idea further and suggested a home-and-home series. He not only sent Wilson east to negotiate with Notre Dame coach Knute Rockne, but he sent Wilson's wife, too, which was probably one of the better moves he ever made as V.P.

"Things were a lot different back then," Wilson recalled in an article in *Pigskin Review*, the USC football program. "You didn't just get on an airplane and fly back to Chicago. It took two days and three nights by train to travel that far. It was quite an undertaking.

"And we didn't depend on a phone either. Had I used a phone to try to set up the game, I probably would have received a polite 'no' from Notre Dame."

The Wilsons took a train to Lincoln, where the Irish were to play Nebraska. They found the personable Rockne surrounded by people in a hotel lobby. He gave them two tickets to the game and told them he could arrange for them to travel back to Chicago with the team, and the series could be discussed then. (Notre Dame was beaten 17-0, and the Wilsons noticed that the people in Lincoln "were very hostile and there was no welcome at all.")

En route to Chicago, Wilson and Rockne stood on the rear platform and talked. "We stood outside that observation car for almost three and a half hours," said Wilson. "The Rock finally decided against a series. He said it was a long way to Los Angeles. His team had been traveling so much that it was being nicknamed 'The Ramblers.' He said Notre Dame could get plenty of games closer at home."

Elsewhere on the train, Marion Wilson and Bonnie Rockne were talking. "I started telling her how well USC treated other teams," said Mrs. Wilson. "I couldn't believe how angry and unpleasant the people in Nebraska had been.

"Without realizing it, I was selling Southern California. It was really a very innocent thing."

The two men rejoined their wives in separate quarters, at which time Mrs. Rockne, in the grand tradition of wives who want to visit sunny climes, started working on her husband. About 20 minutes later, Rockne went ambling down the aisle, casually chatting with people along the way. When he reached the Wilsons, he asked, "Now what did you say about a home-and-home series?" A deal was made, a deal that has lasted 56 years and enriched both schools.

Howard Jones was all for the idea. He and Rockne were not strangers to each other. In 1921 Jones's Iowa Hawkeyes had upset the Irish 10-7 and ended their unbeaten, untied streak at 20 games. Afterward Rockne was quoted as saying, "I want to see a lot more of that fellow. He's got some tricky maneuvers."

The Coliseum was the site of the first game, won by Notre Dame 13-12. The Irish were angry over a 19-0 loss to Carnegie Tech that had spoiled an unbeaten season, but they almost got waylaid again. Their winning touchdown came on an Art Parisien-to-John Niemiec pass in the final seconds. Trojan lineman Jeff Cravath, who had amost blocked Harry O'Boyle's PAT try earlier, did block the last one, but Notre Dame didn't need it, because Morley Drury's extra-point kick had hit the crossbar and the Irish had blocked the other.

A one-point victory, an exciting finish, and

spectacular plays — it was a fitting beginning for a long-lasting sports tradition.

The 1927 game was played before an estimated 120,000 fans at Chicago's Soldier Field (the paid attendance was 99,198, according to the Notre Dame business department), and the Irish again won by a single point 7-6. All-America Morley Drury of Troy was the outstanding back on the field, but Raymond (Bucky) Dahman's PAT made the difference.

1928 — USC earned its first victory 27-14, thanks to the excellent play of backs Don Williams and Russ Saunders and an interception by Francis Tappaan that set up a touchdown. Notre Dame's Jack Chevigny scored on an 81-yard run. It was the last game Rockne ever lost.

1929 — Notre Dame's third one-point victory in four games, 13-12! This time there were 112,192 fans in Chicago's Soldier Field. Saunders returned a kickoff 95 yards. Notre Dame's Frank Carideo set up the tying touchdown and kicked the winning PAT. Rockne had been in bed most of the season suffering from phlebitis, a circulatory disease.

1930 — Notre Dame was one game away from its second-straight unbeaten season, and USC figured to be a tough opponent, especially on its own field. The Trojans had stomped UCLA 52-0, Stanford 41-12, and Cal 74-0, while losing only to Washington State 7-6.

Rockne used two psychological ploys for the game. (No, not his legendary "Win One for the Gipper" speech, in which he supposedly invoked the spirit of star player George Gipp, who had died in 1920.) His first trick was played on his own players before they even arrived in Los Angeles. The team stopped overnight in Tucson, Arizona, and was supposed to have a workout at 9:30 A.M. Rockne purposely canceled the wake-up calls at the hotel. When the last player had straggled onto the field that morning, the coach chewed out the squad, announced he was so disgusted that he was going to leave and check into the Mayo Clinic in Rochester, Minnesota (he had been ill much of the season) and stalked away.

The team proceeded to have a ferocious practice, then sent Frank Carideo to beg Rockne's forgiveness and pledge a dedicated effort to drive the Trojans right out of the peristyle end of the Coliseum.

His second trick was on USC and the press,

switching halfback Bucky O'Connor to fullback, but dressed in the jersey of unknown substitute Dan Hanley. (First-string fullback Joe Savoldi had been expelled for getting married and — worse at the Catholic school — divorced. Second-string fullback Larry Mullins had a leg injury.)

Notre Dame won handily 27-0 before a crowd of 73,967. Marchmont (Marchy) Schwartz, the Jewish Fighting Irishman from Mississippi, passed to Carideo for the first touchdown. O'Connor took a lateral from Marty Brill and went 80 yards for the second, and the new fullback also scored the third.

"There's no doubt about it," said Howard Jones afterward, "that was the greatest Notre Dame team I've ever seen."

It was Rockne's fifth unbeaten season in his 13 years coaching Notre Dame football. He was an American sports hero who had already become legendary even though he was only 43 years old. People were fascinated by him: a Norwegian, yet not tall, blond or Viking-warrior handsome; a fiery, get-down-in-the-dirt-and-show-'em-how-to-block football coach, yet also knowledgeable in Latin and chemistry (he graduated *magna cum laude* from Notre Dame and designed its football stadium); the most famous Notre Dame man of all, yet not a Catholic (until he converted late in his life).

On March 31, 1931, Rockne was a passenger in an eight-passenger, trimotor Fokker, which took off from Kansas City en route to Los Angeles, where he was going to help make a football-demonstration movie. Shortly after takeoff the plane crashed in a Kansas wheat field. All aboard were killed.

1931 — Notre Dame, now coached by "Hunk" Anderson, had won 26 games in a row when USC arrived in South Bend in November to play for the first time in the new stadium in the shadow of the Golden Dome. The Irish went ahead in the second quarter 7-0 on fullback Steve Banas's four-yard run and an extra point. Schwartz, the star for the Irish this day, scored on a three-yard run in the third period, and the PAT made it 14-0.

But USC fought back. In the fourth quarter a Trojan drive ended with Gaius Shaver diving over from the one. Johnny Baker's PAT try was blocked. Notre Dame 14-6. Helped by the second pass-interference call on the Irish in the game,

Johnny Baker

USC drove again from its own 40. At the Irish 10, Shaver took a lateral from Orv Mohler and went around right end to score. Baker's kick was good. Notre Dame 14-13.

With time slipping quickly away, USC continued its tough defense and got the ball again on its own 20. For the third time helped by a pass interference call against Notre Dame, the Trojans moved to the Irish 12. Ray Sparling lost a yard on his specialty, the end-around play. With seconds left, Jones sent field-goal kicker Homer Griffith into the game, but Mohler waved Griffith off and called for Baker to try the kick from the 23. It was good and USC won 16-14, the school's greatest victory up to that time.

Mohler explained afterward: "Baker and I have been practicing that play all year."

Wrote Arch Ward in the *Chicago Tribune:* "A point-scoring whirlwind from the University of Southern California today ended Notre Dame's three-year reign as monarch of American football. Trailing by two touchdowns at the end of the third quarter, the champions of the Pacific Coast swept up and down the field in the closing moments of play to win one of the most brilliant victories in gridiron history, 16 to 14."

Later, Ward, the man who invented the Golden Gloves and Silver Skates competitions, said, "That 1931 battle between Notre Dame and the Trojans was the most thrilling football game I ever saw."

In Chicago, a hat dealer excited by the USC heroics, outfitted the entire team with derbies. A huge crowd gave the Trojans a New York-style ticker-tape parade when they got home to Los Angeles; the huge headline in the *Los Angeles Evening Herald* read, "S.C. HEROES WELCOMED BY CHEERS OF 300,000." The game film drew big crowds to Loew's State Theater downtown. When Braven Dyer and Dick Nash brought out their book, *Ten Top Trojan Football Thrillers*, in 1949, the 1931 Notre Dame game was Thriller No. 1.

1932 — In the Coliseum, 101,000 people saw USC win its nineteenth straight game 13-0. Irvine (Cotton) Warburton was Troy's running star; Notre Dame lost despite having 13 first downs to USC's six.

1933 — USC won its third straight in the series 19-0 and gave the Irish their first losing season since 1888. Warburton scored twice. (Even though Notre Dame beat Army 13-12 in its final game of the season, Anderson was replaced by Elmer Layden, one of the fabled "Four Horsemen" backs of 1922, 1923 and 1924.)

1934 — The Trojan-Irish series stood at 4-4. Notre Dame broke the deadlock with a 14-0 victory before 50,000 people at the Coliseum. Coach Layden's kid brother Mike scored both Notre Dame touchdowns.

1935 — Notre Dame closed out a 7-1-1 season with a 20-13 victory at South Bend. Wayne Millner, Bill Shakespeare, and Wally Fromhart scored touchdowns for the Fighting Irish. This was one of Jones' poorest years: five victories and seven defeats, and two of the victories came at season's end over weak Hawaiian teams.

1936 — The first tie of the series was produced, 13-13. USC earned just *one* first down in the game and that on a penalty, but scored twice on long runs: Lawrence (Bud) Langley zoomed 99 yards with an interception (still a USC record), Dick Berryman zoomed 60 with a lateral. It was the Trojans' third tie of a less-than-mediocre season.

1937 — Notre Dame won 13-7 as Andy Puplis had a 58-yard touchdown run from punt formation.

1938 — "On the record of past performances and achievement the thing looks like a pushover for Notre Dame," wrote one sports-page seer. "Undefeated, untied in nine games against representative opponents of the nation, the Irish should be 1-5 in the wagering." But USC broke the Irish two-season win streak at 11 games with a 13-0 victory, just one of many times that one team robbed the other of a possible national championship.

With four seconds left in the half, quarterback Ollie Day and end Al Krueger hooked up on a 52-yard touchdown pass play that was all USC needed. Hundreds of cards in the Trojan rooting section went flying, ruining the halftime card stunts. Mickey Anderson also scored for USC.

1939 — USC won the fourteenth renewal of the rivalry 20-12. Ambrose (Amby) Schindler ran wild for the Trojans.

1940 — More than 85,000 fans in the Coliseum saw the Irish win 10-6. Notre Dame's Bill Earley batted down a Trojan pass near the goal line in the final seconds. Fullback Milt Piepul scored all the Fighting Irish points, including three on a 25-yard field goal.

1941 — Elmer Layden resigned as football coach and athletic director at his alma mater early in the year to become the first commissioner of the National Football League. He was replaced by another Rockne pupil, Frank Leahy, hired away from Boston College. Howard Jones had died and been replaced for one year by Sam Barry. Not long before the Japanese staged their sneak attack on Pearl Harbor, Notre Dame won at South Bend 20-18, Steve Juzwik's toe providing the margin.

1942 — More than 95,000 people — many of them, as usual, part of Notre Dame's "subway alumni" — saw the Irish win 13-0 behind the passing of Angelo Bertelli, a product of Milt Piepul's old high school in West Springfield, Massachusetts.

1943 through 1945 — No games were scheduled because World War II restricted travel.

1946 — One of the greatest Notre Dame teams of all time — Johnny Lujack and Terry Brennan in the backfield, George Connor and Jim Martin in the line (not to mention Leon Hart, Emil Sitko, Ziggy Czarobski, plus backup quarterbacks George Ratterman and Frank Tripucka) — mopped up on USC 26-6 in South Bend. Only a scoreless tie with a powerful Army team marred the Irish record, and they won their fifth national championship.

1947 — Jeff Cravath's sixth Trojan team was undefeated, but the Irish were loaded with talent again. Before another throng (104,953) in the Coliseum, Notre Dame won a second-straight national title 38-7 and went ahead 12-6-1 in the series. Notre Dame led only 10-7 at halftime, but on the first scrimmage play of the third period Emil (Six-Yards) Sitko became Seventy-Six-Yards Sitko, going 76 yards off right tackle to a touchdown, and the rout was on.

1948 — A crowd of 100,571 saw Notre Dame preserve an undefeated season by tying the Trojans 14-14. It was one of those unsatisfying "moral victories" for USC, because the Irish had been heavily favored. The game had two stirring Irish plays: Leon Hart was hit by Jay Roundy, Don Doll, Art Battle, and Boyd Hachten but just kept plowing toward the end zone until he made the score; with 2:35 left, Billy Gay took a kickoff and went 85 yards to the Trojan 12, setting up Sitko's tying touchdown.

"That team could have played any team in the country to a standstill," said Leahy. "I've never seen a better coached team more ready mentally than the Trojans were against us."

1949 — In South Bend, how could the Trojans stand a chance against such Irishmen as Zalejski, Zambrowski, Zancha, and Zmijewski — plus Sitko, Hart, and Bob Toneff? Notre Dame won 32-0, and Cravath still had not coached a victory over Notre Dame.

1950 — According to longtime Trojan observer Braven Dyer, Cravath "did one of the great defensive coaching jobs of USC history to upset the Irish" 9-7 before 70,177 fans in the Coliseum. Johnny Williams had an important interception for the Trojans and Jim Sears returned a kickoff 94 yards. It didn't save Cravath's job; he was fired a few days later. USC had won only one other game that season.

1951 — Jess Hill took over for Cravath, but he was not to have much better luck with Notre Dame than Cravath. Freshman quarterback Ralph Guglielmi — a master of the option pitchout — led the Irish to a hard-fought 19-12 triumph.

1952 — USC's fine team, led by such stars as Elmer Willhoite, Jim Sears, punter Desmond

Koch, and end Tom Nickoloff, was 9-0 when it traveled east to shivery, snow-frozen South Bend and lost 9-0. John Lattner, the tough Chicago back who didn't seem to mind playing on tundra, scored on a one-yard plunge for the Irish, and Bob Arrix kicked a short field goal.

1953 — Notre Dame romped 48-14 behind the running of Heisman Trophy winner Lattner, Neil Worden, and Joe Heap, who had a 94-yard punt return.

1954 — Another Irish long run, Jim Morse's 72-yarder in the fourth quarter, helped saddle Jess Hill with his fourth straight loss in the series 23-17.

The 1954 win put Notre Dame comfortably ahead in the series 17-7-2, but USC, unlike some other oft-pounded rivals on Notre Dame's schedule, wasn't inclined to cancel the series. From 1955 through 1981, it was not nearly so comfortable for the Irish. Their present margin is 27-21-4.

The USC-UCLA sports rivalry has no match anywhere. They are two large, famous universities in the same city — one private, one public — which together have won 111 national championships in nine men's sports. Privately endowed, USC has won 71 (football eight, baseball 11, gymnastics one, swimming nine, tennis 12, track and field 28, volleyball two). UCLA, the largest campus in the vast University of California chain, has won 40 (football one, basketball 10, tennis 13, track and field five, volleyball eight, water polo three).

Crosstown tension reaches its peak the week of the Biggest Game, the football meeting of the two schools in their mutual home stadium, the Los Angeles Memorial Coliseum. Yale-Harvard is considerably older but seldom means much more to the rest of the country than the Oxford-Cambridge crew race. Cal-Stanford, the "Big Game," is 37 years older (it started in 1892) but seldom means much outside the Bay Area. USC-UCLA is almost always televised nationally. Often at stake are the conference championship and the Rose Bowl bid, and sometimes the game has a strong bearing on the *national* championship as well. But even if the two teams are lousy, the game captures the imagination of Los Angeles.

"It's not a matter of life and death," said Red Sanders in his days as UCLA coach. "It's a little more important than that."

The buildup is delicious. There are newspaper stories every day. Radio and television sportscasters strain to find unusual angles. The *Daily Trojan* and *Daily Bruin* staffs play each other in touch or flag football (the "Blood Bowl"). The two marching bands do the same.

On the morning and early afternoon of the game, the Exposition Park lawns surrounding the Coliseum are crowded with rooters enjoying tailgate parties and picnics. People are decked out in cardinal and gold (USC) or blue and gold (UCLA) hats, shirts, dresses, pants, coats, and probably underwear.

Buttons, T-shirts, posters, and banners proclaim loyalties or hurl insults: "God is a Trojan," "Darth Vader is a Trojan," "U$C," "Flush Twice, It's a Long Way to Westwood," "Mickey MoUSC," "Ruin the Bruins," "Trojans Always Score," "PUSC," "U.G.L.Y. Bruins," "May the Horse be With You," "Trojan Town," "Don't Toy With Troy," "Trojans Do It in the End Zone," "U Clowns Lost Again."

Inside the stadium, the two vast rooting sections bellow organized insults back and forth across the field and try to drown out the other side's spellouts and traditional yells. The animosity hangs so thick in the air that it is a wonder the TV camera high above in the Goodyear blimp can even get a picture of the field. It is particularly tense in such integrated families as the Caneers of Seal Beach, California. She has LOVE USC license plates, he has LUV UCLA plates. For the Biggest Game, she sits on one side of the stadium with five of their children, he sits on the other side with two.

John Robinson says the feeling he gets on the Coliseum floor is one of spirit but not malice:

"It's a great day for me. Walking around that field seeing the blue and gold and cardinal and gold is very impressive. And I don't feel a lot of rancor in this game. We've had the best of it for a while, perhaps. Maybe if I were on UCLA's side, I would feel a little more rancor. I don't know."

(USC has indeed had the best of it lately. In games in which the Trojans *had* to beat UCLA to go to the Rose Bowl, they have won eight in a row: 1967, 1969, 1972, 1973, 1974, 1976, 1978, and 1979.)

The Coliseum on game day is also a fine place for pranks. In the late 1950s a group of USC students arrived at the stadium early and sat in the UCLA rooting section. They unobtrusively removed the card-stunt instruction cards in a large rectangular area in the upper-left of the section and replaced them with cards of their own devising, then left. At halftime, when the loyal Bruin students sitting in those seats dutifully held up the assigned cards, there was a mini-USC stunt within the UCLA stunt, in contrasting colors.

The UCLA alumni in 1939 bought an old Southern Pacific locomotive bell (it weighed 295 pounds with frame, wheels, etc.). Bruin cheerleaders would ring the bell once for each point scored. After the 1941 Bruin opener in the Coliseum, six members of USC's Sigma Phi Epsilon fraternity helped load the bell onto a truck, then stole the keys. When the bell guardians went to get a duplicate set of keys, the ersatz Bruins drove off with the truck. The vehicle was quickly recovered, but not the bell. It remained hidden for a year, until the student body presidents of the two rivals negotiated a deal whereby the bell would be returned and become the Victory Bell, a trophy for the winner of the game. USC's alumni association agreed to pay half the cost of its upkeep.

The hijinks are not restricted to the Coliseum, of course. In 1937 USC's initials were burned into the grass of UCLA's quad. In 1940 two UCLA fraternity pledges set off USC's pile of tinder near La Brea and Exposition well before a scheduled bonfire and rally. They were caught and one got his head shaved, the other got a Mohawk haircut. UCLA students stole USC's dog mascot, George Tirebiter, from a dog and cat hospital in 1947 and returned him with "UCLA" shaved in his fur. In 1975 USC ruined a giant Westwood rally by distributing a phony cancellation notice on genuine UCLA stationery. The Trojan statue is a prime target; he has been painted innumerable times and is usually wrapped in a giant Baggie the week before the game.

There was an epidemic of pranks in 1958. USC students kidnapped the truck driver delivering the *Daily Bruin* the morning before the game and substituted a phony, satirical issue which featured an editorial singing the praises of private over public education. UCLA students hired a helicopter and tried to dump manure on Tommy Trojan; the statue, however, is next to a tall building and the chopper couldn't get close enough. The manure and accompanying leaflets landed

USC played UCLA for the first time in 1929 and won convincingly, 76-0.

south of the campus in Exposition Park.

The football part of the fun started in 1929 with a Thundering Herd stampede, 76-0. (Said the UCLA yearbook, Southern Campus, "Be it forever remembered that the Bruins were courageous martyrs.") USC gained 735 yards to UCLA's 124, Russ Saunders gained 231 yards and scored three touchdowns — averaging a mere 16 yards a carry. Jess Hill, Gaius Shaver, and Erny Pinckert scored two touchdowns apiece. The Bruins had been in the Pacific Coast Conference just a year, and Braven Dyer wrote after the game, "Personally, I can't see any reason for getting all steamed up just because 45 Southern California players ran up 76 points against poor old Bill Spaulding's willing but impotent athletes."

In 1930 the Bruins were still impotent, but the score was 24 points better, only 52-0. Marshall Duffield scored three touchdowns, Orv Mohler averaged 8.6 yards a carry. The game mercifully didn't resume until 1936.

"The game blossomed into a gridiron natural because of UCLA's rise to a prominent position in the football world," said the *Los Angeles Times* before the resumption. "There is no reason why the annual spectacle should not rank with the California-Stanford game in the north as one of the season's classics."

No reason at all.

1936 — The same two coaches, Howard Jones and Bill Spaulding, had casts of about equal talent in the midst of the Depression. The Trojans were experiencing some down years and the Bruins were still growing up. USC had to come back to earn a 7-7 tie. Quarterback Ambrose Schindler engineered the tying drive, with fullback Jimmy Jones going over from the four in the third period.

1937 — One of the best games of the series. USC's Grenny Lansdell put on an expert running and passing demonstration to help Troy move ahead 19-0, but with nine minutes to play the Bruins fought back. Kenny Washington, just a sophomore, threw two touchdown passes to Hal Hirshon (62 and 45 yards) and USC had to make a stand at its own 15 at game's end to save the victory.

1938 — It was back to courageous martyrdom for UCLA. Washington threw a touchdown pass to Woody Strode (later an actor and pro wrestler), but then Ollie Day, Jack Banta, and Lansdell ran up a 42-7 score.

1939 — Both teams were unbeaten and 103,305 fans came to see the collision. USC's Lansdell fumbled at UCLA's one-yard line in the first quarter; Jackie Robinson tackled him to cause the fumble and Washington fell on the ball. The game remained scoreless until the last minute, when UCLA reached the Trojan three. Three runs gained just one yard and on fourth down Bobby Robertson swatted down a Bruin pass in the end zone. Bob Hoffman and Bill Fisk were among the other Trojan defensive heroes. The game ended in a 0-0 tie, but USC got the Rose Bowl bid because of fewer ties on its record, two to UCLA's four.

1940 — Jackie Robinson was the backfield star for UCLA, running for a touchdown and passing to Ted Forbes for another, but USC's Bobby Robertson returned a kickoff 60 yards, gained 170 yards from scrimmage, and scored three touchdowns in a 28-12 Trojan win.

Robinson, later to be the first black major-league baseball player when Branch Rickey brought him up to the Brooklyn Dodgers in 1947, was a difficult runner to stop and worried the USC coaching staff. "Jackie was awfully quick and fast and could stop and go just like that," recalled Cotton Warburton. "Jones used to put his best defensive man on Jackie, telling him to tackle Robinson whether he had the ball or not."

1941 — Tommy Trojan got one of his early unwanted applications of makeup; some scoundrel decorated him like an Indian brave with blue, yellow, and green warpaint stripes. The game ended 7-7, with Vic Smith scoring for UCLA on a lateral from Bob Waterfield and USC's Robertson scoring on a short run after a 63-yard Trojan drive.

1942 — This was the first game for the Victory Bell and the first UCLA win, 14-7. Wrote the *Daily Trojan*, "In memoriam, Troy's domination over UCLA. Born Sept. 28, 1929, died Dec. 12, 1942." Edwin C. (Babe) Horrell was in his fourth season coaching the Bruins, Jeff Cravath in his first with USC. Mickey McCardle and Norm Verry starred for the Trojans, but a Bob Waterfield-to-Burr Baldwin touchdown pass in the third quarter put UCLA ahead to stay.

1943 — World War II forced changes. The teams played twice, USC winning 20-0 and 26-13 to go ahead in the series 7-1-3. Eddie Saenz, who had transferred to USC from Loyola University to take officer-training courses, had an 86-yard touchdown run in the first game, and Ralph Heywood caught a scoring pass from McCardle.

UCLA led the second game 13-6 but couldn't hold on. Most spectacular play: center Bill Gray blocked a Bruin punt in the first quarter and halfback Gordon Gray (no relation) picked it up at the six and carried it in. Saenz, perhaps the best transfer at Troy since Roy (Bullet) Baker switched over from Santa Clara, scored on a 40-yard run.

1944 — War-curtailed travel forced the intracity foes to play twice again. USC was leading the first game 13-6 with seconds to go when Jim Hardy punted to Johnny Roesch on the Bruin 20. Roesch took it all the way back for his second touchdown in minutes. Bob Waterfield's PAT try hit the crossbar and rolled over for the tie.

Hardy scored twice in the second game and the Trojans played superb defense to win easily 40-13, allowing UCLA to score only in the closing minutes.

1945 — UCLA had a new coach, Bert LaBrucherie, but USC still dominated, winning both games before a combined audience of 181,555. A 50-yard drive in eight plays clinched the first game, 13-6. In the second, USC led 19-0 in the first half and no doubt thought it had the Rose Bowl bid safely locked away, but UCLA battled back to make an interesting game of it before losing 26-15.

1946 — UCLA made the Rose Bowl a second time by edging Troy 13-6. On the last play of the third period, McCardle fielded a punt, was hit hard by Al Hoisch and fumbled. UCLA recovered on the five and three plays later Ernie Case went into the end zone on a quarterback sneak, thrilling the blue and gold partisans among the 93,714 fans.

1947 — USC won the dubious honor of meeting Michigan in the Rose Bowl by beating UCLA 6-0. The lone score: Jim (Mystic) Powers passed

Henry (Red) Sanders

to Jack Kirby for 40 yards. The largest crowd of the collegiate football season, 102,050, was treated to an exciting finish. The Bruins reached the Trojan four. A fourth-down trick pass play didn't work; war veteran Gordon Gray intercepted the throw (the first of Ernie Jones' career) in the end zone with 55 seconds left and carried the ball out to the 15, where USC killed the clock. (In the Rose Bowl, the Wolverines chewed up USC 49-0.)

1948 — A Ray Nagel-to-Bill Duffy touchdown pass tied the score with 45 seconds left in the first half, but USC went ahead to stay on a Dean Dill-to-Jack Kirby touchdown pass play covering 60 yards with one second left. USC won 20-13, its twelfth victory in 18 games.

1949 — UCLA had a new head coach, its seventh, an unknown Vanderbilt grad named Henry (Red) Sanders, an advocate of the single wing, punting on third down, defense, and wry humor. He was to give USC many headaches, but he lost his debut 21-7, as Trojan quarterback Dean Schneider (filling in for the injured Jim

Powers) completed 13 of 26 passes for 127 yards and two touchdowns.

1950 — Sanders had his system fully installed and the Bruins handed USC its worst conference loss in history 39-0. Teddy Narleski scored three touchdowns and UCLA outgained the Trojans 423 yards to 79.

1951 — For the first time in the series, UCLA won a second year in a row, 21-7. Ike Jones scored on a 20-yard end around play and linebacker Donn Moomaw intercepted a Rudy Bukich pass and returned it 20 yards for a touchdown. Sanders' Hoover Dam defense allowed USC only a trickle of rushing, 33 yards.

1952 — The two teams were undefeated and untied, and 96,869 zealots went to the Coliseum to see which would win the PCC title and the trip to the Rose Bowl. It was USC 14-12. The big play was Elmer Willhoite's interception of a Paul Cameron pass, which he returned 72 yards to the Bruin eight. Four plays later Jim Sears passed to Al Carmichael for the winning touchdown.

1953 — The Sanders defense was made of steel again. USC gained precious little yardage and made it into UCLA territory only twice all afternoon before losing 13-0. (The Bruins then lost to Michigan State in the Rose Bowl 28-20.)

1954 — UCLA's first and only national-championship football team (in the UPI poll; AP went for Ohio State) held USC to five yards rushing and won easily 34-0 before 102,548 fans. However, USC went to the Rose Bowl because of the PCC's no-repeat rule of the time (and lost to Ohio State 20-7).

1955 — Jon Arnett returned UCLA's opening kickoff 97 yards for a touchdown, but the play was called back because USC's forward wall had lined up five yards too deep. UCLA won 17-7 for its third straight PCC crown.

1956 — C.R. Roberts gained 102 yards and threw a 14-yard touchdown pass to Hillard Hill as USC won 10-7. The margin of victory was Ellsworth Kissinger's 32-yard field goal.

1957 — Don Long threw for two touchdowns and ran for another as UCLA won 20-9 and Sanders improved his record against USC to 6-3. He died after the season.

1958 — USC was a seven-point favorite but only managed a 15-15 tie when Luther Hayes, an NCAA-champion triple jumper, returned a kickoff 74 yards for a touchdown and quarterback

UCLA's single-wing teams of the early 1950s were classic examples of power football. In 1954, the Bruins shut out the Trojans 34-0.

Tom Maudlin ran for the two-point conversion.

1959 — A disputed pass interference call put the Bruins on the Trojan seven, and Ray Smith scored three plays later. Bill Kilmer was the UCLA running star as the Bruins wrecked USC's undefeated season 10-3.

1960 — The USC team made a mediocre year a little cheerier for new coach John McKay, beating UCLA 17-6 and holding Kilmer to 29 yards. Marlin McKeever was the principal Kilmer-stopper and also caught a touchdown pass from Bill Nelsen.

1961 — Bill Barnes was in his third full season coaching UCLA and won his second USC game 10-7 in the rain. Bobby Smith scored all the Bruin points. USC's Carl Skvarna's 38-yard field goal attempt in the third quarter hit the crossbar and bounced back.

1962 — UCLA held USC scoreless for 50 minutes but lost 14-3. Willie Brown made a sensational leaping catch on the Bruin two-yard line, setting up Ben Wilson's touchdown. Quarterback Pete Beathard led an 82-yard touchdown drive for insurance points.

1963 — Beathard and Brown starred again in an easy 26-6 win before 82,460 fans. Linebacker Damon Bame was brilliant on defense. The game had been postponed a week because of the assassination of President John Kennedy in Dallas.

1964 — Once again it was an easy win for USC, 34-13. Mike Garrett ran well, Craig Fertig passed well, and Dave Moton caught well (four passes for 64 yards and two touchdowns).

By the mid-1960s the tradition of dramatic USC-UCLA battles in the Coliseum was well established, a recurring part of Los Angeles life along with the Tournament of Roses Parade and the dry, hot Santa Ana winds. The stage was set for Gary Beban versus O.J. Simpson, John McKay versus Tommy Prothro, John Robinson versus Terry Donahue — classic games for temporary supremacy in the city, yes, but more importantly for lifelong memories of victory or defeat in the heads of the men good enough to wear the colors of either university.

Gifford's Greatest Game

Cal was riding high in 1951. Coached by Lynn (Pappy) Waldorf and led on the field by such outstanding players as Les Richter and Johnny Olszewski, the Golden Bears were undefeated in 38 regular-season games and were ranked number one in the nation when USC visited Berkeley in October. The Trojans, coached by Jess Hill (who had just succeeded Jeff Cravath), had a smattering of talent, too: future pros Frank Gifford, Jim Sears, and Rudy Bukich in the backfield, and such bruisers as Charley Ane, Elmer Willhoite, and Pat Cannamela — an All-America that year — doing the blocking and tackling. Cannamela, however, was accused of going far beyond mere tackling — twisting and injuring Olszewski's leg on Johnny O's first carry of the game. "Dirty Trojans, dirty Trojans," chanted the Cal rooting section. (Later in the season, UCLA made fun of Pat's homely face by chanting, "Back to the zoo with forty-two.")

Even though Olszewski saw only limited duty after that, Cal led at halftime 14-0, pleasing most of the 81,490 fans. But USC scored three touchdowns in the second half, allowed none, and with Gifford's three PATs upset Cal 21-14. Hill remembered it as the greatest thrill of his football-coaching career, ". . . and it was the first of six straight wins for us over Pappy Waldorf."

Braven Dyer covered the game for the *Los Angeles Times* and practically did a toe dance on his typewriter over Gifford's 69-yard run in the third quarter, calling it "one of the most sensational touchdown gallops in Trojan history." Gifford passed to Dean Schneider for the second touchdown and fullback Leon Sellers battered over for the third. Gifford rushed for 115 yards that afternoon, completed five of seven passes for 59 yards, and twice punted out of bounds around Cal's five-yard line.

Gifford enjoyed one of his finest college games, leading the Trojans to victory after they had trailed 14-0 at halftime. At right, linebacker Pat Cannamela, clutching the football, and halfback Frank Gifford celebrate the 21-14 victory over Cal in 1951.

A Battle Primeval

Jess Hill's second season as head coach was his best. The 1952 Trojans smashed just about every early opponent, edged UCLA 14-12 in the league-championship showdown, and traveled back to South Bend with a 9-0 record. Karl Hubenthal drew a "Perfect Season" cartoon for the *Los Angeles Examiner*: a jigsaw-puzzle picture of a Trojan football player, the puzzle missing only a shamrock-shaped piece labeled "Notre Dame." Alas, the 9-0 Rose Bowl bound Trojans *lost* 9-0 in the 27-degree Indiana chill. (That game is one reason why the game in South Bend every other year is no longer played at wintry season's end.)

Wisconsin, led by All-America fullback Alan Ameche, was the opponent in the Rose Bowl. USC single-wing tailback Jim Sears broke his leg early in the first quarter and was replaced by Rudy Bukich, a transfer from the University of Iowa. In the third quarter, Bukich led Troy on a 73-yard touchdown drive, climaxed by a 22-yard pass play to Al Carmichael. "This was the battle primeval," wrote Maxwell Stiles in the *Los Angeles Mirror*. "It was a throw-back to basic football wherein blocking and tackling, hard running and stout, desperate defensive play held sway. . . ." Sam Tsagalakis barely missed a 23-yard field goal attempt or the final score would have been 10-0. The Badgers came close to tying, but Ameche was caught from behind after dashing 54 yards — nabbed by obscure Frank Clayton, who was playing only because Sears and Landon Exley had been knocked out of action.

Hill became the first man ever to play on and coach winning Rose Bowl teams. It was the Pacific Coast's first Pasadena victory in seven years over the Big Ten champion.

Above: Jim Sears cuts upfield against the Badgers in the first period. Sears injured his leg early and was unable to play further. Rudy Bukich passed to Al Carmichael for the game's only score in USC's first Rose Bowl appearance in five years and its first victory in the game in nine years.

Opposite: Lindon Crow intercepts a third-quarter Wisconsin pass deep in Trojan territory. Crow went on to have a ten-year All-Pro career as a defensive back with the Chicago Cardinals, New York Giants, and Los Angeles Rams.

"Something to Remember"

More than 94,000 fans flocked to the Coliseum on a November Saturday in 1955 to see not only the latest battle of the Trojan-Irish War but also two of the nation's finest backs, Notre Dame's Paul Hornung and USC's Jon Arnett, who were good friends off the field. USC went ahead 21-7 on a fake field goal attempt that ended up as an Ellsworth Kissinger-to-Arnett touchdown pass play. Early in the fourth period USC led only 21-20 when Jim Contratto, who shared time with Kissinger, somehow wiggled away from a horde of Irish pursuers and connected with Arnett on a 64-yard touchdown play. Hornung had been intercepted only five times during Notre Dame's 8-1 season, but playing catch-up in the fourth quarter he threw four interceptions, and Troy won 42-20. Said coach Jess Hill, "The team gave themselves and me something to remember and live for the rest of our lives."

Trojan tackler Doug Kranz closes in on Fighting Irish quarterback Paul Hornung in the 1955 Notre Dame game at the Coliseum, won by USC 42-20. The diamond-shaped emblem on USC's helmets commemorated the university's seventy-fifth anniversary.

Early McKay

Head coach Don Clark hired John McKay away from Oregon to be the Trojan backfield coach in 1959. (Coaching backs and ends on that same staff was a young New Yorker named Al Davis.) One year later, Clark had resigned and McKay, the 37-year-old West Virginia native and former Oregon Duck running back, was picked to take up the reins. McKay was not an immediate candidate for the Football Coaches Hall of Fame. In fact, USC lost its first three games, star lineman Mike McKeever missed the second half of the season because of a head injury, and the final record was a sorry 4-6. Things weren't any rosier in 1961: 4-5-1.

But McKay's staff had been recruiting well: Willie Brown, Hal Bedsole, Pete Beathard, Ben Wilson, Damon Bame, and others became Trojans. USC started 1962 with four straight non-conference victories (the 7-0 win over Iowa was particularly tough), then defeated every league opponent plus Navy and Notre Dame. McKay was named the Football Writers Coach of the Year, beating out Wisconsin's Milt Bruhn, whereupon McKay said, "Isn't it wonderful how much smarter I am this year than I was last season?"

On New Year's day, USC engaged Wisconsin in one of the wildest Rose Bowl games ever. Troy had a comfortable 42-14 lead when Badger quarterback Ron VanderKelen started to pass. Wisconsin scored 23 points in a seemingly endless final period before losing 42-37.

USC finished the 1962 season undefeated and untied — 11-0-0 — and was named national champion. John McKay was on his way.

John McKay began his USC coaching career by recruiting two talented quarterbacks, Bill Nelsen (at left with McKay) and Pete Beathard (shown above in a game against Oklahoma).

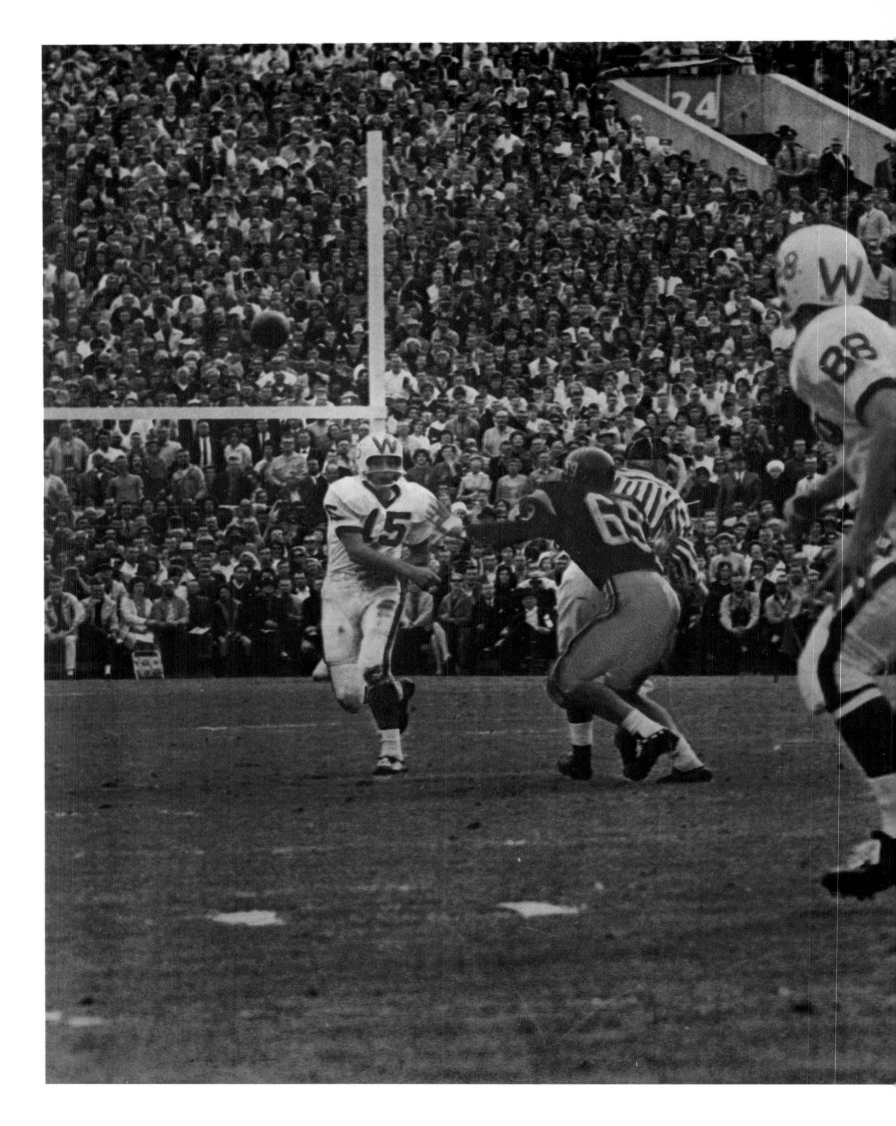

The Ultimate Air War

On New Year's Day 1963, USC played Wisconsin in one of the wildest Rose Bowl games ever, or what one local sports editor called "the most magnificent offensive battle in the 49-game history of Pasadena's . . . classic." USC junior quarterback Pete Beathard completed 8 of 12 passes for 190 yards and four touchdowns, two of the touchdown passes going to Hal Bedsole. Wisconsin's Ron VanderKelen was 33 of 48 for 401 yards and two touchdowns.

USC had a comfortable 42-14 lead in the fourth quarter and seemed to be cruising to a lovely climax to an unbeaten, untied season, its first since the Howard Jones-coached team of 1932. But VanderKelen, who had been ignored in the December NFL draft and selected late by the AFL, started to pass like Sid Luckman and Sammy Baugh combined and scramble like Fran Tarkenton. Time after time, Trojan linemen would frantically chase VanderKelen hither and yon and finally have him cornered, only to see him throw another pass on target. Willie Brown made an interception to stop one drive, but otherwise VanderKelen seemed impossible to contain. It didn't help that one of USC's best defensive linemen, Marv Marinovich, had been tossed out of the game. Wisconsin scored 23 points in an endless final period before losing 42-37 in the twilight of early evening.

There was no exhultation in the Trojan locker room. Halfback Brown was angry: "I'll tell you what happened," he answered reporters. "We won! We relaxed when we got ahead, but we still won.

"Why do people always want to downgrade the Trojans?

"We weren't supposed to win — remember? They were favored and *they* were the Big Ten! We beat them today and it will be the same forty years from now or forty million years from now!"

Wisconsin's Ron VanderKelen, under pressure from USC's Pete Lubisich (69), aims a pass at his big receiver, Pat Richter. Ken Del Conte (20) cannot defend.

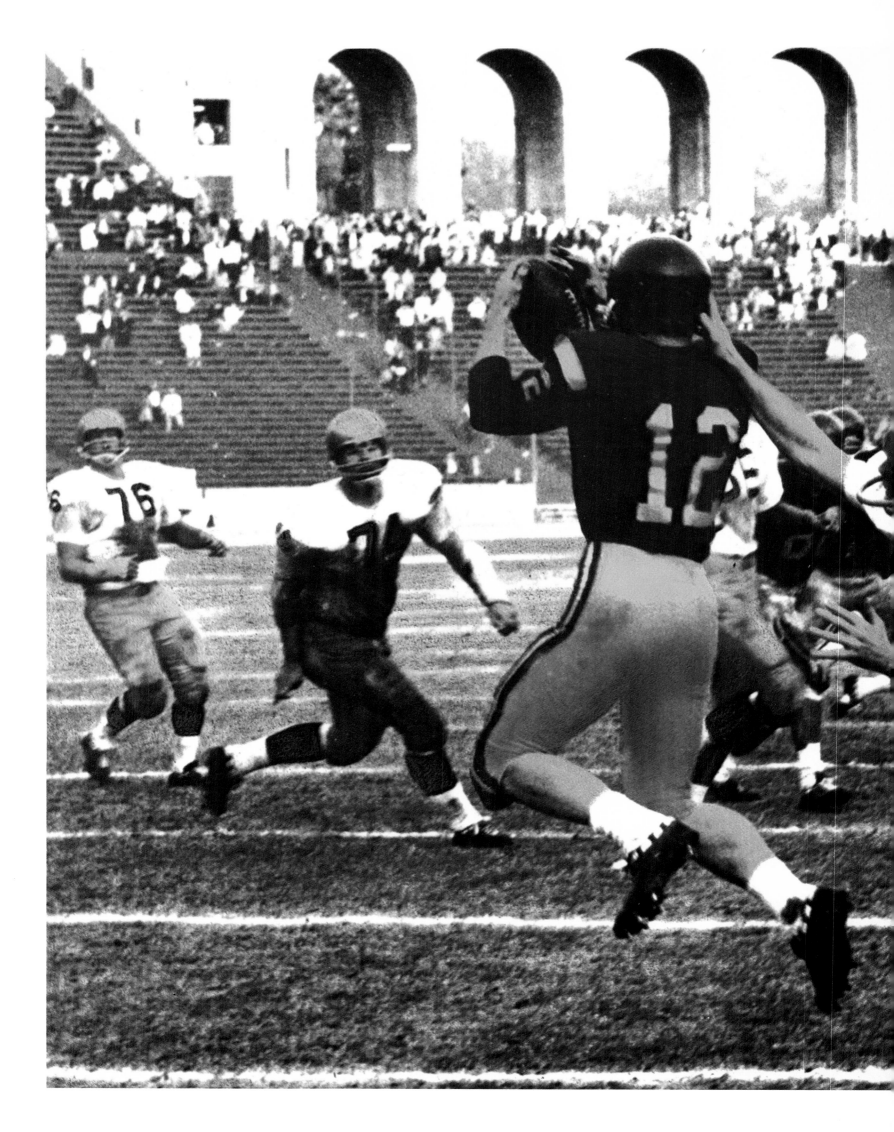

84-Z Delay, But Hold the Roses

At halftime of the 1964 Notre Dame game, USC trailed 17-0. The Irish were ranked No. 1 and were just 30 minutes away from a perfect season. With John Huarte — who won the Heisman Trophy that year — throwing to Jack Snow, who knew how high the score would go? Trojan quarterback Craig Fertig remembered the halftime scene: "Coach McKay told us we could do it, to go out there and take the second-half kickoff to a touchdown and that would be all we needed."

Fertig and friends did just that, but much *more* was needed. Late in the fourth quarter USC trailed 17-13, but, thanks to two Fertig-to-Fred Hill passes, reached the Irish 15. Fourth and eight. Rod Sherman came in with a play he had suggested to McKay — 84-Z delay. He cut in front of a Notre Dame defender on the three, gathered in Fertig's pass and darted into the end zone to climax what just about everyone present (83,840) agreed was the greatest comeback in USC football history. With 1:33 left Huarte almost brought the Irish back but failed.

Some of the immediate joy was taken out of the exciting victory when the conference voted to send Oregon State, not USC, to the Rose Bowl.

Irish defenders Tom Regner (76), Kevin Hardy (74), and Nick Rassas (27) watch helplessly as Rod Sherman leaps in front of defensive back Anthony Carey to take Craig Fertig's pass on the Notre Dame three, and then spin in for the winning touchdown.

The 81 Seconds Explosion

Within 1:21 of playing time in the fourth quarter in 1965, UCLA sophomore quarterback Gary Beban threw two long touchdown passes (to Dick Witcher and Kurt Altenberg), bringing the Bruins from behind to a 20-16 upset victory, the conference championship, and a spot in the 1966 Rose Bowl versus Michigan State. Except for Mel Farr's 49-yard touchdown run in the first quarter, USC had dominated. Senior Mike Garrett — who was to be named winner of the Heisman Trophy — gained 210 yards on 40 carries, and Troy Winslow threw two touchdown passes. But the Trojans also fumbled five times and didn't recover any of them. And after Beban's first touchdown pass, the Bruins tried an on-side kick that worked (linebacker Dallas Grider fell on it). UCLA had lost to Michigan State during the regular season but beat the Spartans in Pasadena 14-12.

Mike Garrett, on his way to winning the Heisman Trophy, straight-arms Bruins linebacker Dallas Grider. A week later, following a resounding victory over Wyoming, Garrett (20) was the center of attention as the Trojans of 1965 gathered for a farewell ceremony.

Defensive tackle Kevin Hardy seems to be taking great pleasure from the rout of the Trojans.

How does a man feel when his arch-rival is beating him 51-0? Lousy. This is John McKay on the sideline watching the Fighting Irish massacre Troy in 1966.

Opposite: Denis Moore (71) and Adrian Young (50) chase Notre Dame's Nick Eddy in the humiliating 51-0 loss to the Irish in 1966.

51-0

Toward the end of the most heavily covered non-bowl game in many years, Notre Dame played for a tie against Michigan State in 1966 and got it, 10-10. There was much criticism of Notre Dame coach Ara Parseghian, including one wag's new Fighting Irish motto: "Tie one for the Gipper." Unfortunately for USC, Notre Dame visited the Coliseum the following week, anxious to prove to the critics and pollsters that it deserved the No. 1 ranking.

The carnage was awful. Coley O'Brien, a sophomore quarterback substituting for injured Terry Hanratty, completed 21 of 31 passes for 255 yards and three touchdowns. Sophomore end Jim Seymour caught 11 passes for 150 yards and two touchdowns. The Irish defense — led by seniors Alan Page and Jim Lynch — allowed the Trojans across the 50-yard line only three times all afternoon. Halftime score: 31-0. Final score: 51-0. Both Associated Press and United Press International voters were impressed enough and Notre Dame got its top ranking.

It was the worst drubbing USC had ever received, worse even than the 49-0 loss to Michigan in the 1948 Rose Bowl or the 35-0 loss to March Field in 1943. The ease with which O'Brien marched his troops was astounding considering that USC had allowed just 63 points in the previous nine games.

John McKay never forgot the licking. His record against Notre Dame the rest of his USC career: 6-1-2. USC's record against the Irish since that game: a spectacular 10-2-2 through 1980.

97

For All The Marbles

The USC-UCLA battle on November 18, 1967 was for the Victory Bell, the conference title, the Rose Bowl bid, and the national championship, and as if the nationally televised game needed any more spice, Trojan O.J. Simpson and Bruin Gary Beban were the main contestants for the Heisman Trophy. Simpson had quite a supporting offensive cast that included tackle Ron Yary and fleet wide receiver Earl McCullouch. The defense had future pros Tim Rossovich and Adrian Young, plus a quick sophomore defensive end, Jim Gunn. UCLA, however, was ranked no. 1 in the wire-service polls; USC had been upset the week before by Oregon State.

Simpson gave USC a 14-7 halftime lead, taking a pitchout 13 yards and dragging two Bruin tacklers over the goal line. But Beban was brilliant, too. He completed 16 of 24 passes for the day, and his two touchdown passes, to George Farmer and Dave Nuttall, put the Bruins ahead 20-14. Zenon Andrusyshyn's extra-point try was blocked by Bill Hayhoe. Bruin fans among the 90,772 people in the Coliseum might have seen that miss as a portent of doom. . . .

UCLA's Gary Beban takes a snap from center in the Bruins' 21-20 loss to USC in 1967.

Guard Steve Lehmer leads interference for O.J.

98

Above: Early in the fourth quarter, Bruin end Dave Nuttall eludes Pat Cashman (30) and Gerry Shaw (46) to score on a 20-yard pass from Gary Beban. The touchdown put the Bruins ahead 20-14.

Right: Bruins kicker Zenon Andrusyshyn prepares to add the point-after-touchdown, but USC's 6'8" defensive end, Bill Hayhoe (85), leaps high to block the kick (sequence at right), holding UCLA's margin to six points.

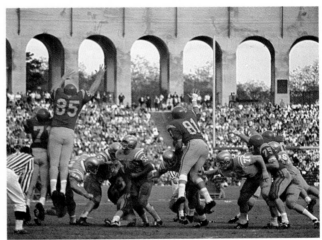

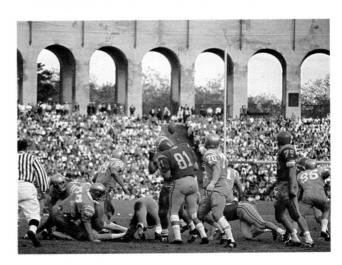

O.J.'s Run

Today O.J. Simpson is retired from pro football and restricts his flying to Hertz commercials on TV. On that important Saturday in 1967 he decided to turn on his jets in the fourth quarter on the Coliseum turf. Bill Becker of the *New York Times* described what happened after the blocked UCLA point after touchdown: "Within one minute, Simpson broke away at the Trojan 36 on a swing around left end. He outran the secondary by cutting back over the middle at about the Bruin 40. With Earl McCullouch, the star hurdler and flankerback, shading off potential tacklers, O.J. rambled all the way without being touched." Quite considerate of John McKay to provide a 13.7 high hurdler to run interference for a 9.6 sprinter. After the 64-yard run tied the game 20-20, Rikki Aldridge won it with his third extra point.

"I don't think I've ever seen a quarterback play better than Gary did against us," said McKay later. "I think you saw two of the greatest players in college football out there — Beban and O.J. Simpson."

Senior Beban won the Heisman over junior Simpson, but all the other marbles went to USC.

O.J. Simpson prepares to cut sharply left at the start of the 64-yard touchdown run that sealed USC's 21-20 victory over UCLA. Tackles Mike Taylor (74) and Ron Yary (77) are the frontline troopers who have already made their blocks. On the left, tight end Bob Klein (84) is about to knock down another Bruin defender.

Rikki Aldridge kicks the winning extra point.

O.J. Sniffs the Roses

USC closed out its fifth national-
championship season (the second
under John McKay) with a 1968 Rose Bowl
victory over Indiana 14-3. A record
Pasadena crowd of 102,946 saw what sports
writers like to call a "defensive struggle"
but which was really a dull game. O.J.
averaged 5.1 yards a carry, had a 27-yard
run nullified by a clipping penalty, and
scored both Trojan touchdowns on short
runs. The USC defense conducted frequent
raids on the Hoosier backfield, throwing
quarterback Harry Gonso for 37 yards in
losses. Said Gonso afterward, "Their front
four was the toughest I've ever played
against. And their defensive backs were
awfully quick. I had to release the ball a
little faster than I wanted to sometimes and
that put me off target."

Indiana coach John Pont was impressed
with the Trojan defense, too, but most of his
praise went to O.J.: "If you put Simpson on
any other ball club that we've played, they
would be the best team."

Allison Danzig in the New York Times *called him "incredible" and "the
greatest running back of the year" — and O.J. Simpson indeed put on a
show in the Rose Bowl on New Year's Day 1968. He gained 128 yards on
25 carries and scored both Trojan touchdowns.*

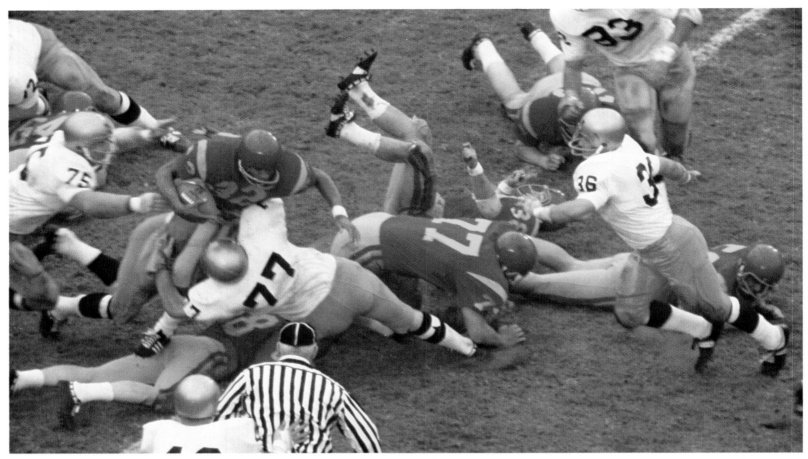

Notre Dame defensive end Bob Kuechenberg (75) and defensive tackle Mike McCoy (77) join in bringing down Simpson in the 21-21 tie in 1968. It was the final game of the season and Simpson's last in the Coliseum as a Trojan. At right, he salutes the USC cheering section during the postgame celebration.

Theismann as in Heisman Meets Simpson as in O.J.

USC was 9-0 late in 1968 and rated No. 1 by UPI, but it had not been awesome against most opponents. Stanford had fallen by three, Washington by seven, Oregon by seven, Oregon State by four. Then Notre Dame held O.J. Simpson to his lowest yardage total in two years, 55, and led at halftime 21-7 behind the fine all-around play of quarterback Joe Theismann. But Trojan quarterback Steve Sogge had one of his best days (17 of 28 passes for 187 yards). His 40-yard touchdown pass play with Sam Dickerson (plus Ron Ayala's PAT) tied the game at 21. And Sandy Durko, Gerry Shaw, and Mike Battle in the Trojan secondary made four interceptions. Scott Hempel barely missed a last-minute 33-yard field goal for the Irish. "Other teams playing against O.J. have made that one big mistake," said Ara Parseghian. "And we didn't."

O.J. Simpson finds the going rough against the Buckeyes.

A Bouquet of Thorns

Ohio State's grumpy Woody Hayes brought a talented group of sophomores to the Rose Bowl in 1969: quarterback Rex Kern, halfback John Brockington, middle guard Jim Stillwagon, rover Jack Tatum. Kern threw two touchdown passes in the fourth quarter to give the Buckeyes a 27-16 win and spoil USC's unbeaten season. O.J. Simpson made his last college game an outstanding one with an 80-yard touchdown run in the second period, a 6.10 rushing average, and eight receptions for 85 yards. But he and quarterback Steve Sogge also fumbled at key times. A few days later, Sogge, who had been captain of both the football and baseball teams, signed a contract with the Los Angeles Dodgers organization. Simpson, already the Heisman Trophy winner, continued to collect honors by the carload, including *Sport Magazine's* Man of the Year award.

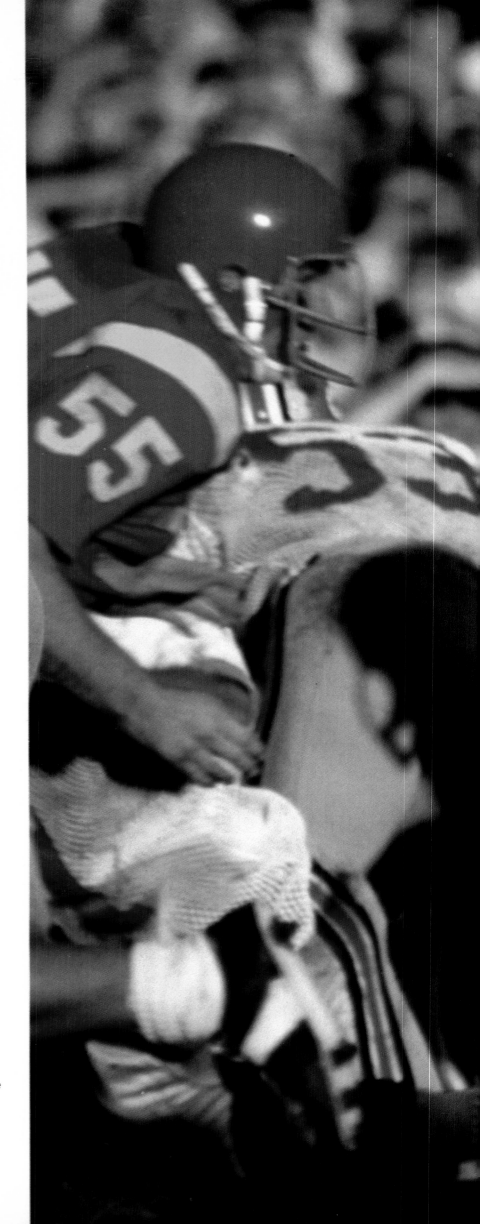

Ohio State teams under Woody Hayes were noted for their battering fullbacks. Here Jim Otis plunges into the USC line during the 1969 Rose Bowl. Linebackers Jim Snow (55) and Bob Jensen (51) penetrate Buckeye blockers to stop him.

Pride and Poise

Stanford had not beaten USC in 11 years, and coaches John Ralston and John McKay despised each other, so it was doubly frustrating to the Cardinals in 1969 (they were the Indians then) when Ron Ayala beat them with a fourth-quarter field goal for the second straight season. This time the junior's 34-yarder barely cleared the crossbar at the gun for a 26-24 win. Quarterback Jim Plunkett starred for Stanford, but cornerback Tyrone Hudson intercepted him just before halftime and returned it 57 yards for a touchdown. Tailback Clarence Davis gained 198 yards and quarterback Jimmy Jones calmly directed the drive to good field-goal position for Ayala.

Six games later more than 90,000 people rocked the Coliseum (groaning or cheering) when Sam Dickerson made a great leaping catch of a Jones pass deep in the end zone with 1:32 left to give the Trojans a wild 14-12 victory over previously unbeaten UCLA. The Bruin goat was Danny Graham, who was called for interfering with Dickerson on a controversial fourth-down pass play that kept the winning drive alive. "I feel like my whole life just went down the drain," said Graham afterward. "I love this team," said McKay a few days later. "I told them that before the game. This is the most interesting team I've ever been associated with. They have two things that are important — pride and poise."

Quarterback Jimmy Jones sprints out and looks for an open receiver in the 14-12 win over UCLA in 1969. Jones completed only five of 21 passes in the game, but one of them was to Sam Dickerson (shown smiling in the locker room) for a 32-yard touchdown with just 92 seconds left in the contest.

The Wild Bunch

Bob Chandler caught a pass from Jimmy Jones on the 10 and made a nice run into the end zone for the deciding (and only) touchdown over Michigan in the 1970 Rose Bowl (final score: 10-3). He was named player of the game, an honor that usually goes to offensive stars, but much more important was The Wild Bunch (self-named after a violent western movie of the day), the defensive line led by Jimmy Gunn, Tody Smith (younger brother of Michigan State All-America Bubba Smith), Charlie Weaver, and Al Cowlings. The Wild Bunch made a miserable afternoon for Wolverine quarterback Don Moorhead and running back Billy Taylor. The defensive backfield wasn't weak either — Sandy Durko dived to intercept a Moorhead pass and that led to the Jones-Chandler touchdown. Life was miserable for Michigan coach Bo Schembechler even before the game started; he was in St. Luke's Hospital suffering from a heart attack and defensive coordinator Jim Young had to direct the Big Ten champion's effort. It was Michigan's first loss in Pasadena in five tries.

Tailback Mike Berry, who had a big high school reputation in Minnesota but didn't play much for USC, is buried under a pack of Wolverines in the 1970 Rose Bowl.

Bob Chandler barrels into the end zone for the only touchdown scored in the 1970 Rose Bowl victory over Michigan. The 100 on Chandler's helmet? The NCAA was celebrating college football's centennial year during the 1969 season.

Edesel Garrison

Pete Adams

Charles Young

1972 Early Season "I'd Like to Have Beaten Them by 2,000 Points"

After two 6-4-1 seasons, the 1972 Trojans were loaded. All-Americas and future pro stars filled just about every position, and it was a confident John McKay who watched practices from his usual perch on a golf cart. The offense had fullback Sam Cunningham, tailback Rod McNeill (soon to be overshadowed by Anthony Davis), tight end Charles Young, wide receiver Lynn Swann, quarterbacks Mike Rae and Pat Haden, and center Dave Brown. Defense had backs Artimus Parker and Charles Hinton, tackles John Grant and Jeff Winans, linebacker Richard Wood and end James Sims. Arkansas fell 31-10, Oregon 51-6, Illinois 55-20 (Davis's first big game). After the Trojans beat Stanford for the first time in three years, 30-21, McKay got riled by a reporter's question that seemed to imply USC had poured it on. "I'd like to have beaten them by 2,000 points," he snapped. "They have no class. They're the worst winners we've ever gone up against." New Stanford coach Jack Christiansen then likened McKay to a skunk.

USC proceeded to trample Cal, Washington, Oregon, and Washington State, and it appeared that it just *might* score 2,000 points against somebody. Troy's record was 9-0, but UCLA and Notre Dame were coming up. . . .

John McKay didn't get close to many of his players, but Pat Haden was an exception. Here they discuss strategy during the 1972 season.

Opposite: Mike Rae

Another Classic Matchup

UCLA came into the 1972 crosstown classic with an 8-1 record and a 5-1 record in conference. But there was no comparison between the two teams. All-America tackle Pete Adams and fullback Cunningham blocked beautifully for Anthony Davis, who had a 6.85 rushing average and, in the first half alone, 112 yards, including a 23-yard touchdown run. Rae completed 7 of 12 passes for 95 yards and Swann made three catches for 61. Linebacker Wood was in on 18 tackles. The Trojans won 24-7 to earn a Rose Bowl bid and few in the crowd of 82,929 were surprised. "This was such a long time coming," said guard Allan Graf, a senior. "I'm so proud, so happy, I'm in seventh heaven."

Above: Tight end Charles Young happily displays a rose after USC beat UCLA 24-7 to clinch the Rose Bowl bid in 1972.

Opposite: Lynn Swann displays his inimitable style against UCLA.

115

Six Times Six For Davis

At the start of the 1972 season the most prominent college backs in the Los Angeles area were Terry Metcalf of Cal State Long Beach, Kermit Johnson and James McAlister of UCLA, and Rod McNeill and Sam Cunningham of USC. Behind McNeill was Allen Carter, probably the fastest tailback McKay ever had. But by midseason, sophomore Anthony Davis was a Trojan star. And in the 45-23 victory over Notre Dame that clinched No. 1 for USC in both wire-service polls, he was incredible.

AD scored six touchdowns that day and set a school record for all-purpose running — 368 yards (99 rushing, 51 receiving, 218 returning kickoffs). He took the opening kickoff 97 yards to a touchdown. When sophomore quarterback Tom Clements brought the Irish back to 23-25, Davis raced 96 yards to a score with the subsequent kick-off. Often there was Cunningham ahead of him, knocking down defenders like tenpins.

"They were big and tough in the middle," said Davis. "But I knew that on returns I would break for the outside if I didn't see our middle wedge hold up. I've always liked to sweep."

"His stride is long and unusual," McKay told the *New York Times*. "Sometimes he seems to have that skip in midair like Gale Sayers. He's well-muscled and an aggressive runner. He challenges the tacklers and is strong enough to break away from them. After all, he was a citywide wrestling champion as a schoolboy. . . . He also was chosen the football player of the year as a left-handed quarterback and the baseball player of the year as a left-handed outfielder."

Sophomore Anthony Davis (left) races to one of his six touchdowns against Notre Dame in 1972. "I've never had a day like it," he said. The Coliseum scoreboard tells the story of an incredible afternoon.

AD's TDs

Here's a score-by-score breakdown of Davis' great six touchdown afternoon against Notre Dame in 1972:

He took the opening kickoff 97 yards to a touchdown, breaking the USC record of 95 shared by Russ Saunders, Don Doll, and Aramis Dandoy. Later in the first period he scored on scrimmage runs of one and five yards to put Troy ahead 19-3.

Charles (Sugarbear) Hinton intercepted a Clements pass and three plays later Davis carried the ball in from the four. A 26-yard pass play, Mike Rae to Lynn Swann, set up the touchdown run.

The Irish got to within two points and it seemed USC was in trouble, but Davis's 96-yard kickoff return broke Notre Dame's spirit. AD added an eight-yard touchdown run in the fourth quarter, set up by Artimus Parker's interception.

"Anthony Davis is the greatest I've ever seen on kickoff returns in college," said Notre Dame coach Ara Parseghian.

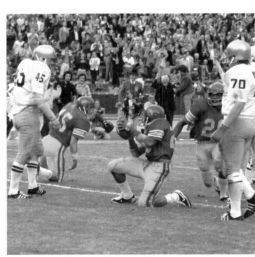

"We knew he was good," said Notre Dame coach Ara Parseghian of Anthony Davis. "We contained him pretty well at the scrimmage line, but our defensive game plan broke down on kickoffs."

"My Greatest Team"

Ohio State had just won its fourth Big Ten title in five years and its 1973 Rose Bowl team had six future first-round NFL draft choices (including freshman Archie Griffin), which is perhaps why the Buckeyes were able to tie USC the first half 7-7. Then Davis, Rae, Swann, Young, and company went to work and won with ease 42-17. Davis had a 20-yard, tackle-busting touchdown run, and Sam Cunningham scored four touchdowns on short flights over line pileups. It was John McKay's third unbeaten season, and a marvelous year for new assistant John Robinson. "There's no doubt it was my greatest team," McKay claimed later. "As Nebraska's Bob Devaney said, it will go down as one of the greatest of all time. I know I've never seen a team that could beat it — if the kids played as well as they could play."

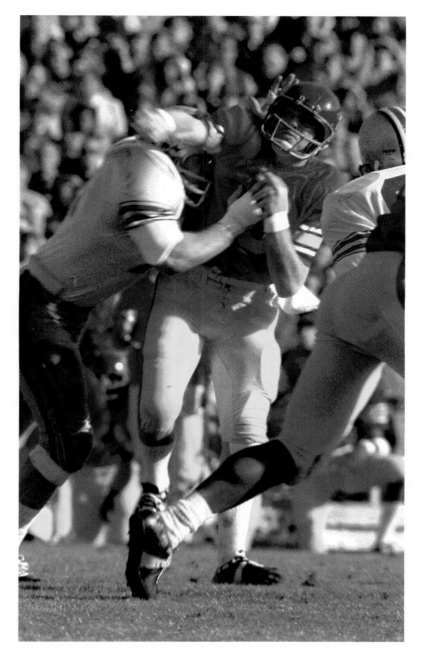

Mike Rae gets off a pass just before being clobbered.

Sam (Bam) Cunningham takes off on another flight into the end zone against Ohio State. Sam scored four touchdowns, a record for the New Year's Day classic.

Opposite: Ohio State's freshman tailback Archie Griffin, destined to win two Heisman Trophies, is stopped by a phalanx of Trojans defenders, among them Charles Phillips (49), Marvin Cobb (24), and Artimus Parker (14).

121

The String Ends at 23

Few groups in the world — and that includes dervishes and women scorned — can be whipped to a frenzy like a Notre Dame student body or a Notre Dame football team. On October 27, 1973, the Irish, who hadn't beaten USC in six years, shook down the thunder (and some drizzle) in South Bend and stopped the Trojans and Anthony Davis 23-14. Notre Dame's nation-leading defense held John McKay's power-I running attack to a lower-case-i 68 yards. Davis, who had run for six touchdowns versus the Irish the year before, had just 55 yards in 19 carries. (One campus sign implored, "Our Father Who Art in Heaven, Don't Let Anthony Davis Score Seven.") Three field goals by Bob Thomas and a third-period 85-yard scoring run by junior Eric Penick were enough to win the game. USC's unbeaten string was broken at 23 games; the streak had started on the same field in 1971. Notre Dame, with such specimens as tight end Dave Casper, defensive tackle Mike Fanning, and defensive back Luther Bradley, went on to win the national championship.

Notre Dame freshman Ross Browner, who was to see two of his younger brothers play for USC in the 1980s, chases Pat Haden in the 1973 Trojan-Irish skirmish, won by Notre Dame 23-14.

Cracking the Wishbone

The 1973 UCLA press guide touted coach Franklin Cullen (Pepper) Rodgers Jr. as "the Westwood Wizard of the Wishbone." His wishbone attack was indeed formidable that year, for the Bruins went into the annual crosstown match as three-point favorites, with a 9-1 record and an average of 415 yards a game on the ground, most prolific in the nation. But USC's defense, led by middle guard Monte Doris (who had 18 tackles), held Kermit Johnson, James McAlister, and Co. to 249 yards. UCLA hurt itself with two interceptions and four lost fumbles.

USC's scores came on a four-yard sweep by Davis, a 16-yard Pat Haden-to-J.K. McKay pass play, and Chris Limahelu field goals of 32, 35, and 28 yards. (The 5-5, 137-pound soccer-style kicker, of Indonesian descent, had earlier in the season kicked a 34-yard field goal with three seconds left to beat Stanford 27-26.) Davis made 145 yards in 27 carries to become only the second Trojan ever to have consecutive 1,000-yard seasons. (O.J. Simpson was the first.)

The final score: USC 23, UCLA 13. Coach John McKay would be taking a team north on the Pasadena Freeway to the Rose Bowl for the seventh time in 11 years.

Opposite page: Anthony Davis cracks the UCLA line for some of the 145 yards he gained against the Bruins in 1973.

Left: In a moment of pure joy, Pat Haden holds aloft his good friend and battery-mate, J.K. McKay, following a touchdown against the Bruins.

125

Ohio State fullback Pete Johnson scored three touchdowns and, at right, pulls away from Charles Phillips and Gary Jeter. Woody Hayes, the Buckeyes' coach, storms onto the playing field in the fourth period, exhorting his players.

Woody's "Greatest Victory"

After Ohio State and Michigan tied 10-10 in their annual season's-end war, and tied for the Big Ten championship, the conference voted to send the Buckeyes to Pasadena, despite the fact that Woody Hayes's team had made the trip the year before. Wolverine coach Bo Schembechler and the entire state of Michigan howled, but it proved to be a prudent decision. Ohio State scored 28 points in the last 20 minutes to beat USC 42-21. Even with such horses as Steve Riley and Booker Brown blocking up front, USC was held to just 167 yards rushing. Woody claimed that he had worked extra hard on his passing attack, but legwork by fullback Pete Johnson (three touchdowns), Archie Griffin (a 47-yard touchdown run), and Neal Colzie (56-yard punt return) hurt Troy much more. "This is the greatest victory I have ever had," said Hayes.

Bruins halfback Russell Charles goes down in the 1974 Big Game as Trojans defensive back Charles Phillips moves in. Phillips intercepted 13 passes in his USC career.

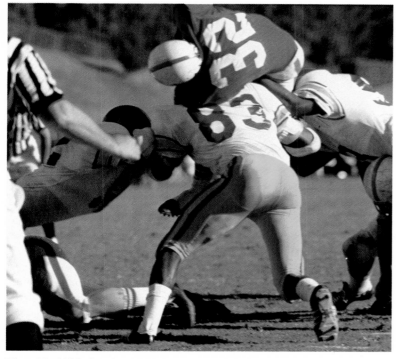

The 1974 USC-Stanford game was a showdown for the Rose Bowl bid, and USC won easily 34-10. Art Riley, Gary Jeter, and Richard Wood helped the Trojans defense stifle the vaunted Cardinals attack. Here Wood stops Stanford Fullback Dave Tenn.

Opposite: Anthony Davis eyes another long run during the 1974 national championship season. J.K. McKay (25), so often a target of Pat Haden's passes, helps clear the way for AD.

Two Stumbles en route to No. 1

USC won its seventh national football championship in 1974 (according to UPI voters anyway) despite being soundly beaten 22-7 at Arkansas in the season opener and tied by California in the seventh game. John McKay was optimistic about the team's chances from the beginning and well he should have been. Anthony Davis was back for his senior year, about 15 pounds lighter. Linebacker Richard Wood was back and feeling stronger for having given up vegetarianism. Quarterback Pat Haden and receivers J.K. McKay and Shelton Diggs gave Troy a dangerous passing attack. Sophomore fullback Ricky Bell and linemen Marvin Powell and Donnie Hickman provided powerful blocking. The defense had such prime athletes as Gary Jeter up front and Danny Reece and Marvin Cobb in the secondary.

It was a spectacular season. Davis returned a kickoff 106 yards versus Arkansas, 80 versus Iowa. Defensive back Charles Phillips returned two midair fumbles 83 and 98 yards to touchdowns against Iowa (in the statistics they counted as interceptions). Haden's passing was disappointing at times, but he had two touchdown passes against Oregon State and two more against Washington.

In the ninth game Davis zipped over 1,000 yards for the third straight year. In the tenth, a 34-9 stomping of UCLA, he gained 195 yards on 31 carries and had a 46-yard touchdown run from scrimmage that brought the 82,467 fans to their feet. Once again USC had earned the right to represent the West in the Rose Bowl, with one small item of business to take care of first — Notre Dame.

1974 Notre Dame
Notre Dame Wins the
First Half 24-6 ...

At his Munch with McKay continental breakfast a few days before the 1974 Notre Dame game, the gray-haired coach marveled at the Irish defense, which was statistically the best in the country at the time. "They do not leak, they submerge *you*," he said, and added, "You're not going to make a lot of points on them." A *Sports Illustrated* writer at that breakfast was a bit disgruntled. He had originally been assigned to do an Alabama-Auburn cover story but had been taken off it and told to do a few paragraphs on USC-Notre Dame for the *Football's Week* roundup. He didn't dream he'd get a fold-out cover.

The first half was no contest. Notre Dame seemed to move when it felt like it. A 39-yard drive to a touchdown, a 79-yard drive to another, a field goal, a Tom Clements touchdown pass. It was 24-0, but USC got on the scoreboard just before halftime. Pat Haden passed the team down the field and hit Anthony Davis with a little swing pass for a touchdown. The extra point attempt was smothered by the center of the Irish line.

"I thought McKay did a great job at halftime of talking about being calm,"

recalled John Robinson. "Everything in our dressing room was calm. He told the team, 'We are really a very good football team. That wasn't *us*. If we can just go out and be us and believe in ourselves and just do what we do instead of worrying about the score or worrying about them.' No storming at all. Very confidence-building."

Top: Notre Dame quarterback Tom Clements runs the option against USC in 1974. Clements had a fine game — 14 pass completions for 180 yards and a touchdown — but the No. 1-ranked Irish defense was embarrassed by USC's 55 points.

Above: Quarterback Pat Haden and coach John McKay confer in the waning moments of the first half with USC trailing the Irish by 18 points.

Opposite: Notre Dame was absolutely delighted when AD used up his eligibility. Here he flies to one of his two touchdowns against the Irish in the remarkable 1974 game in the Coliseum.

Ara Parsegian can't believe his eyes.

1974 Notre Dame . . . USC Wins the Second Half 49-0

Davis received the second-half kickoff two yards into his end zone and ran it back all the way, starting what *Sports Illustrated* called "one of the most remarkable scoring blitzkriegs in college football history and the worst disaster for the Irish since the potato famine." In less than 17 minutes — counting the touchdown pass just before halftime — USC scored eight touchdowns and 55 points. This against America's best defensive team.

In little more than one quarter Davis scored 26 points, Haden completed eight of eight passes for 144 yards and four touchdowns, J.K. McKay caught four for 110 yards and two scores, Charles Phillips intercepted two passes and returned them 83 yards, Kevin Bruce recovered two fumbles and, as *SI* pointed out, Notre Dame coach Ara Parseghian "contemplated hara-kiri with a yard-line marker."

"If someone with a crystal ball had told me beforehand what was going to happen," said Haden, "I would have said, 'Put that guy away.' It was pure fantasy." Especially for Davis, who ended up with 11 touchdowns and 68 points against the Irish in three games. But no Heisman Trophy. Most of the ballots had been filled out and mailed before the game.

By scoring 55 points in less than 17 minutes, USC had plenty to celebrate. Among the revelers here: offensive tackle Steve Knutson (77), flanker Shelton Diggs (26) hugging Anthony Davis who had just scored, split end J.K. McKay (25), and tight end Jim O'Bradovich (89).

Above: Buckeye fullback Pete Johnson barrels into the USC line, which held him to no touchdowns and only 33 net yards.

Opposite: USC's defense had its problems containing Buckeye quarterback Cornelius Greene, but here it stops the Ohio State running attack with no gain, with defensive backs Charles Phillips, Danny Reece, and Marvin Cobb leading the charge.

One More Miracle

Ohio State went into the 1975 Rose Bowl with a 10-1 record, a Heisman Trophy-winning tailback in junior Archie Griffin, and enough talent at other positions to start a pro franchise in Columbus. And, of course, cantankerous Woody Hayes. Despite the fact that USC had scored an astounding 55 points against Notre Dame, the odds-makers favored the Buckeyes by 5½ points. A crowd of 106,721 fans was on hand, anxious to compare Griffin with Troy's Anthony Davis.

But Davis was injured in the first half and saw no action in the second. Before he left the scene, he fumbled deep in his own territory. Ohio State capitalized on the error, scored, and led 7-3 at halftime. After a scoreless third period, USC took the lead in the fourth on a Pat Haden-to-Jim Obradovich touchdown pass but fell behind 17-10 due to an 82-yard scoring drive by the Buckeyes and Tom Klaban's 32-yard field goal. Late in the game — six minutes to go — USC took possession on its own 17. With Davis on the sideline nursing sore ribs, a miracle seemed unlikely. . . .

Haden to McKay One Last Time

Haden didn't start flinging desperation passes. Substitute tailback Allen Carter broke loose for a 30-yard run, fullbacks Dave Farmer and Ricky Bell made important gains, and the Trojans marched to the Buckeye 38. First and 10. Earlier J.K. McKay, Haden's target for so many touchdown passes in high school and college, had run a corner pattern into All-America Neal Colzie's territory, and Colzie had intercepted the pass. This time the Trojans sent McKay into the territory of a mere mortal, All-Big Ten Steve Luke. McKay got behind Luke in the right corner of the end zone, where Haden hit him with a pass that traveled more than 50 yards. Ohio State 17-16. USC, as usual, went for the win instead of the tie. Haden rolled out right and passed to Shelton Diggs, who did a combination dive-kneel-sprawl to make the catch. USC 18-17. And that's how it stayed.

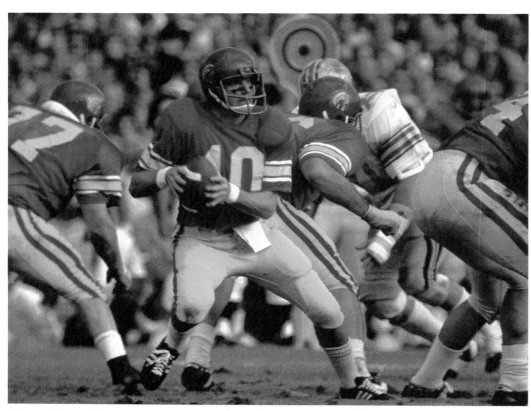

Above: Rhodes Scholar Pat Haden drops back to pass in the 1975 Rose Bowl game versus Ohio State. Haden's 38-yard touchdown pass to J.K. McKay tied the game 17-17.

Opposite: Shelton Diggs sprawls in the end zone after diving to catch Pat Haden's game-winning two-point pass in the 1975 Rose Bowl. Defender Neal Colzie (20) turns away as J.K. McKay begins to celebrate.

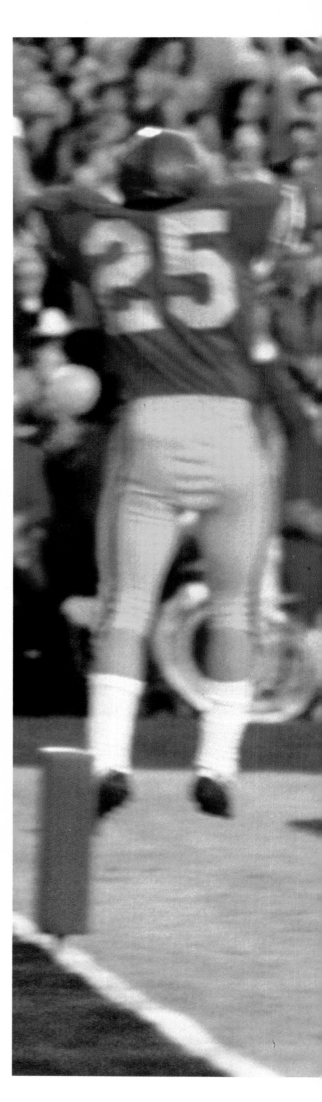

John McKay was to have his troubles later in the 1975 season, his last at the Trojan helm, but here he's enjoying an October afternoon in South Bend, watching USC stay undefeated with a 24-17 victory over arch-rival Notre Dame. Ricky Bell (right) battered the Irish for 165 yards.

McKay's Last Season

Three times USC trailed at South Bend in 1975 and three times it fought back, the last time with a 71-yard touchdown drive in the fourth quarter. Mosi Tatupu had a big day at fullback, but the hero was ex-linebacker, ex-fullback Ricky Bell, who carried 40 times from his new tailback spot for 165 yards and a touchdown. He made 47 of the 71 yards on the winning drive and prompted Irish coach Dan Devine to say, "He's as good as any back I've ever seen. He can take punishment, which is what makes O.J. so great. He never seems to tire." Wrote Rick Talley in the *Chicago Tribune*, "The Fighting Irish — and they were courageous — simply wore down in the final quarter against 215-pound Ricky Bell, 225-pound Mosi Tatupu and their brigade of mammoth blockers." Final score: USC 24, Notre Dame 17.

Robinson's Debut

After 16 seasons at the helm (and at the wheel of his practice-field golf cart), John McKay had moved across the continent to Tampa Bay in 1976. His successor, John Robinson, announced that he wanted to make the quarterback position more important at USC. With the help of quarterback coach Paul Hackett, he kept his word. However, in his head coaching debut, it was *Missouri's* quarterback, Steve Pisarkiewicz, who starred, along with tailback Curtis Brown. On a stormy, rain soaked Saturday night, the Tigers shocked and embarrassed Troy 46-25, the worst opening loss in school history. It was as if a promising young conductor got his chance to lead a fine orchestra, but the music at the first concert sounded like traffic noise.

Well, the orchestra soon got tuned up. USC won its next 10 games, scored 347 points with a balanced running-passing attack (an average of 34.7 an outing) and played steel-walled defense. Rob Hertel threw four touchdown passes against Iowa, and he was only second string behind Vince Evans. Freshman Charles White averaged 5.83 yards a carry and scored three touchdowns versus Oregon State, and he was only Ricky Bell's sub. The indefatigable Bell, a Sherman tank with motorbike mobility, was AP's back of the week for gaining 347 yards on 51 carries against Washington State, a school and conference record.

The defense, featuring tackle Gary Jeter and back Dennis Thurman, dominated the traditional UCLA and Notre Dame battles. The Bruins, unbeaten and averaging 361 yards a game on the ground, could run for only 140 against the Trojans (Bell alone had 146). USC won 24-14. The Irish, wrote Bob Oates of the *Times*, "were in scoring position eight times but misfired six times against clutch defense." USC won 17-13.

Robinson was voted Pac-8 maestro of the year.

Above: John Robinson, who had been an assistant coach for Oregon, USC, and the Oakland Raiders, was hired to replace John McKay in 1976. Here he talks on the sideline with quarterback coach Paul Hackett, whom Robinson hired away from Cal.

Opposite: Ricky Bell dashes for another long gain in the 1976 opener versus Missouri. A strong candidate for the Heisman Trophy, Bell started his campaign with 172 yards on 29 carries, but it was a horrible debut for coach John Robinson — Missouri won 46-25.

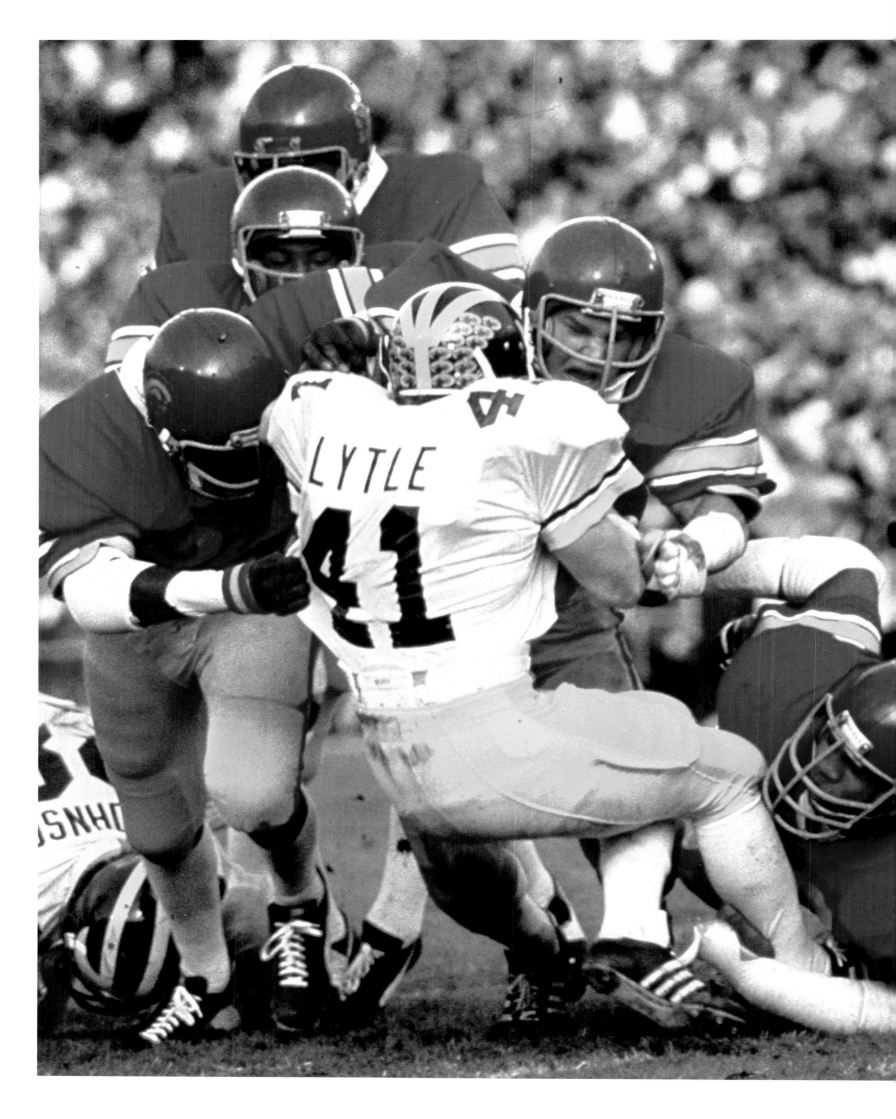

With Ricky Bell sidelined by injury, quarterback Vince Evans responds brilliantly to lead USC's 14-6 victory and win the MVP trophy in the process.

The Big Ten Grounded Again

After five plays, Ricky Bell left the 1977 Rose Bowl game with a mild concussion and did not return. It was not an auspicious beginning for the Trojans, especially when the opponent was Michigan, a team that had held five opponents scoreless and led the nation in total offense, rushing, and scoring. But it also was a team that could not pass well enough in the clutch — typical of the Schembechler-Hayes squads that had represented the Big Ten in Pasadena so often. Sophomore quarterback Rick Leach had thrown for 13 touchdowns during the season, but he completed only four of 12 this New Year's Day. The USC defense, honed by John Robinson and assistants Marv Goux, Foster Andersen, Don Lindsey, and Bob Toledo, held the Wolverines to one skimpy touchdown (eight less than they had scored against poor Navy). Final score: USC 14, Michigan 6. (Michigan's PAT attempt was blocked by Walt Underwood.)

Both of USC's touchdowns were set up by long passes from quarterback Vince Evans, who was much improved over the season before, when he had completed only 31 percent of his tosses. The Trojans ran well, too. Charles White took over for the injured Bell and gained 114 yards on 32 carries, scoring the team's second touchdown on a seven-yard run in the final period. Fullback Mosi Tatupu, described by Robinson as "as hard to tackle as a Coke machine," took time out from blazing trails for White and averaged 8.7 yards on seven carries.

USC's win improved its Rose Bowl record to 15-6. The Big Ten, once so dominant, had lost nine Rose Bowl games in the last 12 years. And this was the first one to John Robinson, Troy's rookie head coach.

Opposite: On this play in the 1977 Rose Bowl game, Michigan tailback Rob Lytle finds rushing against the USC line is a bit like running uphill against an avalanche. Bringing him down, left to right: David Lewis, Clay Matthews, and Gary Jeter, with Dennis Thurman and others coming up fast.

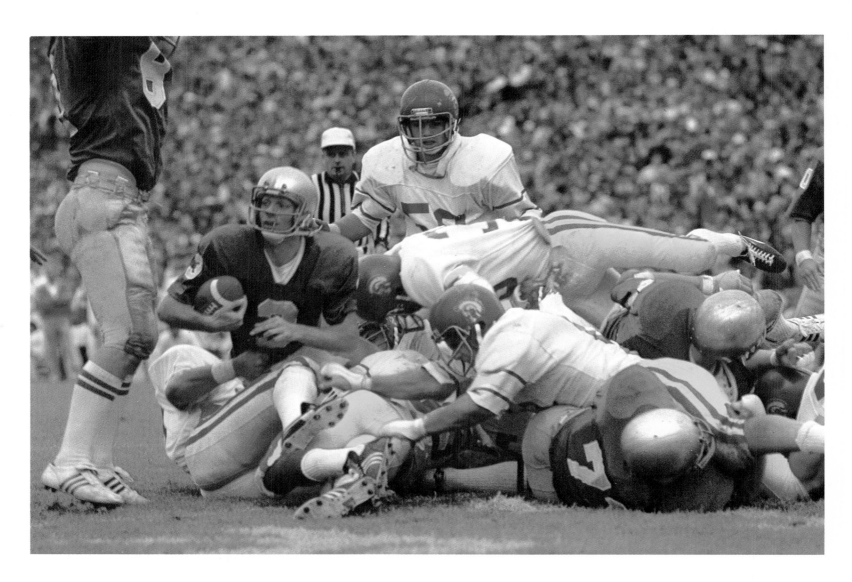

Fighting On

The 1977 USC-UCLA game had everything: scoring, comebacks by both sides, exciting plays, controversy, and — more than any mile race — a big finishing kick. Quarterbacks Rick Bashore of the Bruins and Rob Hertel of the Trojans had fine days (five touchdown passes and 390 passing yards between them). UCLA jumped off to a 10-0 lead, but USC led at the half 17-10 and after three quarters 26-17. Near the end of the fourth quarter UCLA was back on top 27-26. A questionable pass-interference call on Bruin safety Johnny Lynn helped Troy get to the UCLA 19, fourth down and six. Two seconds left. In came placekicker Frank Jordan.

"We've practiced running it with no time outs left and executing, so we didn't have any problems," said Jordan, a transfer from UC Riverside who had missed two PAT tries earlier in the game. "All I remember is that it was a great snap by Mike McDonald, a great hold by Mike Carey, and I hit it solid and it took off straight." The ball sailed 38 yards and through the uprights, giving USC the victory 29-27 and Jordan joined Johnny Baker, Sam Tsagalakis, Ron Ayala, and Chris Limahelu in the Trojan placekicking pantheon.

Top: The USC defense swarms over Notre Dame quarterback Joe Montana. In a pregame surprise, Irish coach Dan Devine presented his underdog squad brand new kelly green jerseys. The psychological ploy worked: The Trojans were embarrassed 49-19 in a nationally televised game.

Robinson is obviously involved in the game at South Bend.

Opposite: Rob Hertel rolls to his left in the 1977 UCLA game. The senior quarterback passed for three touchdowns in the Trojans' 29-27 win.

Forging a solid four-game winning streak to start the 1978 season, USC then traveled to Tempe, Arizona, for a date with Arizona State. On a hot desert night, the Trojans played turn-over to the Sun Devils and suffered their only loss of the season, 20-7. Above, Arizona State defenders celebrate a fumble recovery as Trojans players look on in disbelief.

A Dream Deferred

Alabama upset No. 1-ranked USC in the Coliseum in 1977, so it seemed only fair when John Robinson's Trojans returned the favor in 1978 before a record crowd of 77,313 at Legion Stadium in Birmingham. Alabama was favored by 10½ points, perhaps because (a) USC was going with an unproven quarterback, Paul McDonald, and (b) the Tide had done such a good job of containing tailback Charles White the previous year, and (c) Paul "Bear" Bryant seldom loses at home.

USC never trailed in the game. McDonald proved himself a worthy successor to Rob Hertel by completing nine of 16 passes for 113 yards and two touchdowns, and frequently changing signals at the line of scrimmage. Behind the bulldozer blocking of Anthony Munoz, Pat Howell, Lynn Cain, Brad Budde, and others, White gained 199 yards on 29 carries, a shocking 6.86 average. The secondary contributed four interceptions. "We were just out to physically dominate them," said Munoz, the 6-7, 280-pound concrete slab of a tackle. "It was nothing fancy — just our basic offense."

Few if any spectators that hot day dreamed that Alabama, whipped 24-14 in its own backyard, would be picked over USC by one poll for the national championship at season's end.

USC was a 10½-point underdog going into the 1978 Alabama game in Birmingham's Legion Stadium, but as the Los Angeles Times headline read the next morning, "White Lays the Groundwork (199 Yards) for Upset." Troy won 24-14 and White had a 40-yard scoring run to account for some of those 199 yards on Bear Bryant's sacred turf.

Two-Second Warning: Here Comes Mr. Jordan

The Trojans finished the 1978 regular season as the fine team John Robinson had predicted it might become. Nose guard Rich Dimler and the rest of the defense once again made a prolific UCLA running attack look pathetic: 62 yards. Over the season USC had outscored the opposition 103-6 in the second quarter; against the Bruins it was 14-0. The 17-0 halftime lead held up for a 17-10 victory, junior tailback Charles White ran for 145 yards, and junior quarterback Paul McDonald threw two touchdown passes. It was USC's sixth victory in seven years over its Los Angeles neighbor.

At first the Notre Dame game was easier. The Trojans led 24-6 at the end of three quarters. But Fighting Irish quarterback Joe Montana led his team to three fourth-period touchdowns. A pair of two-point conversion tries failed, and Notre Dame led 25-24. McDonald claimed later that he was not at all worried. "We had two time outs, and all we had to do was get into field-goal range," he said. "We were in great shape." Starting at his own 30,

McDonald quickly moved USC into Irish territory. There were two key plays. One was a 35-yard pass to Calvin Sweeney. The other was a critical call. Notre Dame tackle Jeff Weston smashed into McDonald and jarred the ball loose, but the referee, despite vigorous protests from the Irish, ruled it was an incomplete pass, not a fumble.

With two seconds left, John Robinson sent in kicker Frank Jordan, just as in the previous year versus UCLA. Jordan was in danger of being the goat, because he had missed a PAT and a short field-goal attempt earlier in the game. In the gathering darkness he kicked a 37-yard field goal to beat the Irish 27-25.

Above: Marty King hugs placekicker Frank Jordan just after the San Franciscan's 37-yard field goal beat Notre Dame in the final two seconds 27-25. The Irish had made a great comeback in the 1978 game, scoring three touchdowns in the fourth quarter.

Opposite: UCLA quarterback Rick Bashore finds it is not easy to see your target when Ty Sperling (63) and Charlie Moses (55) are bearing down on you with mayhem on their minds.

149

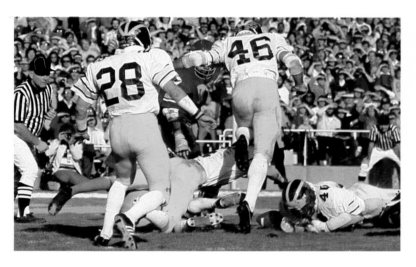

1979 Rose Bowl I
The Phantom
Touchdown

The second quarter belonged to USC all season. And so it was in the 1979 Rose Bowl struggle with Michigan. The Trojans led 7-3 in the second quarter when tailback Charles White dived *a la* Sam Cunningham over the maize and blue, cardinal and gold pileup and onto paydirt. Touchdown!, signaled line judge Gilbert Marchman (from the Big Ten). But White was emptyhanded when he landed; Wolverines were swarming over the ball at the one. Most observers of the TV replay thought White had been stripped of the ball by linebacker Ron Simpkins before he entered the end zone, but Marchman's call stuck. Said Michigan linebacker Jerry Meter after the game, "The ball hit the ground on the one-yard line and just stayed there. It never got in." At the half it was USC 17-3.

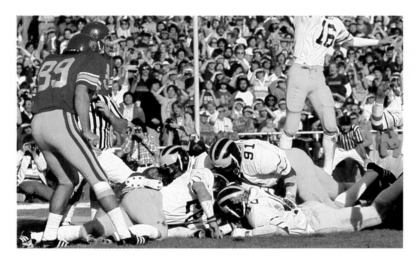

USC beat Michigan 17-10 in the 1979 Rose Bowl, but the TV replay of Charles White's second-quarter touchdown seemed to show he fumbled the ball before he scored. "The line judge saw the ball break the plane [of the goal line]," said Referee Paul Kamanski. "The line judge was emphatic and in perfect position."

1979 Rose Bowl II

The second half of the 1979 Rose Bowl consisted of two excellent teams playing tenacious defense. Quarterback Rick Leach threw a touchdown pass for Michigan in the third period, but USC held tight for a 17-10 victory. This was a defensive feat of some proportions, because the Wolverines had averaged almost 33 points a game during the season and had been held below 20 only twice — never below 14. Among the USC heroes: All-Coast nose guard Rich Dimler, a tough guy from New Jersey; all-conference linebacker Dennis Johnson (from Flint, Michigan!), who led the team in tackles for the second straight year, and defensive backs Ronnie Lott and Dennis Smith.

The Sporting News and UPI awarded the national championship to USC (its eighth). AP, the National Football Foundation, and the Football Writers Association gave it to Alabama. Michigan's Bo Schembechler, phantom touchdown or not, voted for USC.

Above: Michigan coach Bo Schembechler and USC's John Robinson meet amid the post-game chaos on the field in 1979. Bo manages to smile despite having just lost his second New Year's Day game to Troy in three seasons.

Opposite: Lynn Cain spent much of the 1978 season blocking for Charles White, but he became a running star in the 1979 Rose Bowl, carrying the ball 14 times and averaging 6.43 yards.

The Great White Way

USC was unbeaten in 1979, John Robinson's fourth year as head coach, but was tied by Stanford when the Cardinals roared back from a 21 point deficit. Cardinal quarterback Turk Schonert completed 14 of 22 passes in the second half and had a hand (or feet) in three touchdowns scored in the last 20 minutes, running for one and passing for two. "We froze in the second half," said Robinson, and defensive coordinator Don Lindsey added, "We were missing tackles as much as anything. We got tired, we made mistakes — two face-mask penalties."

The next week the Trojans traveled to Notre Dame for the nationally televised renewal of their old rivalry. It was one of the most entertaining games in the series and gave Charles White a big boost toward beating out Oklahoma's Billy Sims for the Heisman Trophy. He carried the ball 44 times for 261 yards, four touchdowns, and a 5.93 rushing average. The first half was a 7-7 defensive battle, then the fireworks started: a 22-yard touchdown run by Notre Dame's Vagas Ferguson, a Paul McDonald-to-Kevin Williams pass on third and 10 that gained 41 yards, a 23-yard run by White on USC's final touchdown drive. Eight touchdowns in two quarters. The Trojans won 42-23.

Washington fought hard before falling 24-17, but UCLA, a 15-point underdog, got stomped into a Bruin rug, 49-14. The score was 35-0 at halftime, McDonald passed for 199 yards, and White rushed for 194. Charlie's four touchdowns gave him 52 for his career. Said Bruin coach Terry Donahue, "We got licked by a vastly superior team, one that is extremely well coached."

Above: Stanford fought USC to a 21-21 draw in the Coliseum at midseason, putting the only blemish on the Trojans 1979 record. Brad Budde (71) and Marcus Allen lead Charles White against the Cardinals.

Below: Following the UCLA game, Charles White leaves the Coliseum field for the final time in a Trojan uniform.

Opposite: Marcus Allen was the second I-formation back to serve an apprenticeship as a fullback before moving to the glamour position, tailback (Ricky Bell preceded him). Here the San Diego-bred star blocks for Charles White against Notre Dame in 1979.

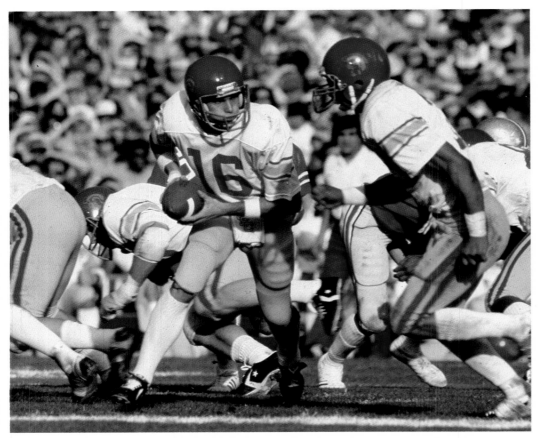

Quarterback Paul McDonald passed for 234 yards in the 17-16 victory over Ohio State.

1980 Rose Bowl: Chapter I

Curmudgeon Woody Hayes had been ousted from the Ohio State coaching job for striking an opposing player, but Columbus was no less a football capital with Earle Bruce calling the shots. The Buckeyes went into the 1980 Rose Bowl with an 11-0 record and a dangerous passer-runner in sophomore quarterback Art Schlichter, UPI's Big Ten player of the year. USC, hardly feeble either, had Heisman Trophy winner Charles White and, clearing paths for him up front, Lombardi Trophy winner Brad Budde. Plus a fairly good coach of its own in John Robinson, who announced on the eve of the game that he had signed a contract to stay at the school five more years.

"There's just so much emotion in college football," he said, "and I haven't had enough of it yet."

January 1, 1980 generated about half a contract's worth of emotion. USC jumped off to a 10-0 lead on a 41-yard Eric Hipp field goal and a typically flamboyant Paul McDonald-to-Kevin Williams touchdown pass play, this one covering 53 yards. Ohio State got even on Vlade Jankievski's 35-yard field goal and a Schlichter touchdown pass to Gary Williams. A third-period Jankievski field goal and another field goal in the fourth quarter put the Buckeyes up 16-10.

USC found itself on its own 17-yard line with 5:21 to play. Many worried Trojan rooters, remembering Pat Haden to J.K. McKay or even ancient history, Doyle Nave to "Antelope Al" Krueger, prayed for Paul McDonald to unlimber his arm. . . .

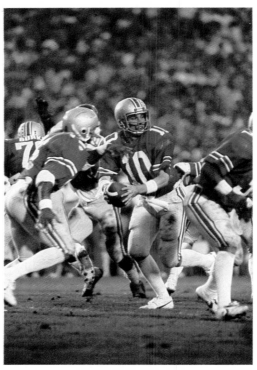

Art Schlichter, Ohio State's sophomore quarterback, passed for 297 yards in a brilliant performance.

Dennis Edwards (70) and Chip Banks (51) are joined by an unidentified Trojan as they sack Buckeyes quarterback Art Schlichter in the second half.

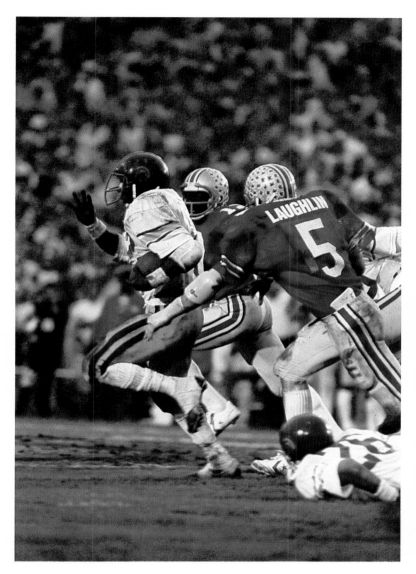

In the postgame locker room, White and McDonald answer questions while clearly displaying the strain of the hard-fought contest.

1980 Rose Bowl: Chapter II

With 83 yards to go and a fair amount of time, USC decided to go with its ground forces. In this case, the I in I-formation stood for infantry. And what troops the Trojans had: Brad Budde, Marcus Allen, Roy Foster, Keith Van Horne, and others blasting open holes for White, statistically the second-best rusher in college-football history.

White over right guard for 32 yards. White around right end for 28 more. Michael Hayes for seven. Fullback Allen for five down to the Ohio State 11. Then White for three, for five, for two and, finally, one yard over the top for the tying touchdown — and this time he kept the ball. Hipp's PAT made it USC 17-16, which held up when Ohio State failed to get a first down and McDonald used up the remaining time. USC had won its sixteenth Rose Bowl game in 22 tries, and John Robinson was three for three.

Opposite/Above: In the closing minutes Charles White took command of the game, gaining 71 yards of an 83-yard drive. The tremendous display ended with White catapulting to the winning touchdown and, at left, he leaves the field, the ball held high in victory.

In the Big Game, linebacker Steve Busick intercepts against UCLA, but the Bruins, behind All-America tailback Freeman McNeil, won in the fourth quarter 20-17.

A Melancholy Season

Because of Pac-10 penalties, USC was not eligible for a bowl appearance at the end of the 1980 season. Adding to that unhappy situation, the Trojans lost two in a row, to Washington and UCLA, and went into the finale with Notre Dame minus their star tailback, Marcus Allen, and their quarterback, Gordon Adams, both out with injuries. And this wasn't just any crop of Fighting Irishmen. Dan Devine's last Notre Dame team was 9-0-1 — only a 3-3 tie with Georgia Tech blemished their record — and was very much in the running for a national title.

Yet USC won — won with what John Robinson, perhaps a little intoxicated with victory, called "the greatest defensive exhibition I've ever seen." Junior linebacker Chip Banks (who made a terrific interception and returned it 49 yards to the one), safety Ronnie Lott (USC's MVP that season) and the rest of the defensive unit held Notre Dame to one first down in the first half, no touchdowns, and just 120 yards total. Final score: 20-3.

It was the fifth time in the 52-year history of America's greatest intersectional rivalry that USC had spoiled an unbeaten season for Notre Dame and knocked the Irish out of a possible national championship. The Trojans' record since losing 51-0 in 1966: 10-2-2.

Above: Joey Browner (47) watches teammate Dennis Smith make a spectacular interception against Notre Dame in the 1980 game, won by USC 20-3. Robinson called it "the greatest defensive exhibition I've ever seen."

Right: With Marcus Allen injured and unable to play, sophomore tailback Anthony Gibson carries the attack to the Irish.

Stu
Bo
Rig

dent

ly

ht

ALL-TIME ALL-AMERICA SELECTIONS

This is a complete list of USC football players who have been named to All-America *first* teams. In recent years, the only All-America teams recognized by the University's sports information office have been Associated Press, United Press International, Football Coaches Association, Football Writers Association, and Walter Camp Foundation.

No.	Year Name & Position	1st Team	2nd Team	3rd Team	Consensus
1	1925 Brice Taylor, G	2	0	0	
2	1926 Mort Kaer, B	9	0	0	X
3	1927 Morley Drury, B	10	1	0	X
4	1927 Jesse Hibbs, T	8	1	0	X
5	1928 Jesse Hibbs, T	3	0	2	
6	1928 Don Williams, B	2	1	0	
7	1929 Nate Barragar, G	1	1	0	
8	1929 Francis Tappaan, E	5	4	0	
9	1930 Garrett Arbelbide, E	1	2	0	
10	1930 Orv Mohler, B	1	1	1	
11	1930 Erny Pinckert, B	9	1	0	X
12	1931 Johnny Baker, G	9	1	0	X
13	1931 Erny Pinckert, B	4	0	1	
14	1931 Gus Shaver, B	6	0	1	X
15	1931 Stan Williamson, C	2	0	0	
16	1932 Tay Brown, T	1	5	2	
17	1932 Aaron Rosenberg, G	1	1	1	
18	1932 Ernie Smith, T	10	0	0	X
19	1933 Aaron Rosenberg, G	8	2	0	X
20	1933 Irvine Warburton, B	10	0	0	X
21	1938 Harry Smith, G	3	2	2	
22	1939 Grenny Lansdell, B	2	1	1	
23	1939 Harry Smith, G	10	0	0	X
24	1943 Ralph Heywood, E	6	0	0	X
25	1944 John Ferraro, T	10	1	0	X
26	1947 Paul Cleary, E	7	1	0	X
27	1947 John Ferraro, T	5	4	0	
28	1951 Pat Cannamela, LB	4	3	0	

Pat Howell

No.	Year Name & Position	1st Team	2nd Team	3rd Team	Consensus
29	1951 Frank Gifford, B	1	1	1	
30	1952 Jim Sears, DB	6	0	0	X
31	1952 Elmer Willhoite, G	8	0	0	X
32	1955 Jon Arnett, B	3	3	0	
33	1959 Ron Mix, T	1	1	1	
34	1959 Dan Ficca, T	2	0	1	
35	1959 Marlin McKeever, E	4	0	1	
36	1959 Mike McKeever, G	1	3	1	
37	1960 Marlin McKeever, E	1	5	1	
38	1962 Hal Bedsole, E	10	0	0	X
39	1962 Damon Bame, LB	2	0	0	
40	1963 Damon Bame, LB	3	1	1	
41	1964 Bill Fisk, G	2	2	0	
42	1964 Mike Garrett, TB	2	2	0	
43	1965 Mike Garrett, TB	11	0	0	X'H
44	1966 Nate Shaw, DB	8	1	1	X
45	1966 Ron Yary, T	8	3	0	X
46	1967 O.J. Simpson, TB	11	0	0	X'
47	1967 Ron Yary, T	11	0	0	X'
48	1967 Adrian Young, LB	9	2	0	X
49	1967 Tim Rossovich, DE	5	2	0	X
50	1968 O.J. Simpson, TB	10	0	0	X'H
51	1968 Mike Battle, DB	3	2	1	
52	1969 Jimmy Gunn, DE	8	1	0	X
53	1969 Al Cowlings, DT	3	1	0	
54	1969 Sid Smith, T	4	2	0	
55	1969 Clarence Davis, TB	1	1	1	
56	1970 Charles Weaver, DE	6	3	0	X
57	1971 John Vella, T	4	1	0	
58	1971 Willie Hall, LB	2	2	0	
59	1972 Charles Young, TE	8	0	0	X
60	1972 Richard Wood, LB	2	2	0	
61	1972 Sam Cunningham, FB	2	0	0	
62	1972 Pete Adams, T	1	2	0	
63	1972 John Grant, DT	1	2	0	
64	1973 Lynn Swann, FL	6	0	0	X
65	1973 Richard Wood, LB	5	1	0	X
66	1973 Booker Brown, T	4	3	0	X
67	1973 Artimus Parker, DB	4	1	0	X
68	1974 Anthony Davis, TB	6	0	0	X'
69	1974 Richard Wood, LB*	3	0	0	X
70	1974 Charles Phillips, DB	1	0	0	
71	1975 Ricky Bell, TB	5	0	0	X'
72	1975 Marvin Powell, T	1	2	0	
73	1976 Ricky Bell, TB	5	0	0	X'
74	1976 Gary Jeter, DT	2	1	0	
75	1976 Dennis Thurman, DB	3	1	0	X
76	1976 Marvin Powell, T	1	0	0	
77	1977 Dennis Thurman, DB	5	0	0	X'
78	1978 Pat Howell, G	5	0	0	X'
79	1978 Charles White, TB	5	0	0	X'
80	1979 Brad Budde, G	5	0	0	X'
81	1979 Dennis Johnson, LB	1	0	0	
82	1979 Charles White, TB	5	0	0	X'H
83	1980 Ronnie Lott, DB	5	0	0	X'
84	1980 Keith Van Horne, T	3	0	0	X
85	1980 Roy Foster, G	1	0	0	

X — NCAA consensus
X' — NCAA unanimous
H — Heisman Trophy

*Richard Wood was USC's first three-year All-America and the first three-year selectee by AP from the West Coast.

Gaius (Gus) Shaver

Michigan State coach Duffy Daugherty, spokesman for the Kodak All-America Team, poses with 1967 USC honorees, Ron Yary, O.J. Simpson, Adrian Young, and Tim Rossovich.

TROJANS IN COLLEGE FOOTBALL HALL OF FAME

Class	Player, Position
1951	Howard Jones, Coach
1954	Morley Drury, Back
1955	Harry Smith, Guard
1957	Erny Pinckert, Back
1966	Aaron Rosenberg, Guard
1970	Ernie Smith, Tackle
1971	Walter Dan McMillan, Tackle*
1972	Mort Kaer, Back
1974	John Ferraro, Tackle
1975	Frank Gifford, Back
1975	Irvine (Cotton) Warburton, Back
1980	Raymond (Tay) Brown, Tackle

*McMillan was more famous for his play at Cal, which lists him as lettering in 1920 and 1921. USC's sports information office records that he lettered at Troy in 1917 and 1919.

Harry Smith

Aaron Rosenberg

MODERN ALL-TIME COLLEGE FOOTBALL TEAM

Selected by the Football Writers Association of America in 1969. No Trojan was picked for the starting eleven.

First Team

End	Bennie Oosterbaan	Michigan
End	Don Hutson	Alabama
Tackle	Bronko Nagurski	Minnesota
Tackle	Frank (Bruiser) Kinard	Mississippi
Guard	Jim Parker	Ohio State
Guard	Bob Suffridge	Tennessee
Center	Mel Hein	Washington State
Quarterback	Sammy Baugh	TCU
Halfback	Jay Berwanger	Chicago
Halfback	Harold (Red) Grange	Illinois
Fullback	Ernie Nevers	Stanford

Second Team

End	Harold (Brick) Muller	California
End	Leon Hart	Notre Dame
Tackle	Fred (Duke) Slater	Iowa
Tackle	Cal Hubbard	Centenary
Guard	Tommy Nobis	Texas
Guard	Aaron Rosenberg	USC
Center	Chuck Bednarik	Pennsylvania
Quarterback	Johnny Lujack	Notre Dame
Running Back	Tom Harmon	Michigan
Running Back	Doak Walker	SMU
Running Back	O.J. Simpson	USC

50-YEAR ROSE BOWL TEAM

In 1971 a poll of 22 sports writers and Rose Bowl experts was conducted to pick the greatest players from the first 50 years of the Pasadena New Year's Day classic.

Offense

Position	Name	School	Year
End	Don Hutson	Alabama	1935
End	Pat Richter	Wisconsin	1963
Tackle	Bob Reynolds	Stanford	1934-35-36
Tackle	Al Wistert	Michigan	1948
Guard	Aaron Rosenberg	USC	1933
Guard	Alex Agase	Illinois	1947
Center	Mel Hein	Washington State	1931
Quarterback	Jim Plunkett	Stanford	1971
Back	O.J. Simpson	USC	1968-69
Back	Ernie Nevers	Stanford	1925
Back	Buddy Young	Illinois	1947

Defense

End	Bill Daddio	Pittsburgh	1937
End	Monk Moscrip	Stanford	1934-35-36
Tackle	Alex Karras	Iowa	1957
Tackle	Carl Eller	Minnesota	1962
Guard	Jim Stillwagon	Ohio State	1969
Guard	Harry Smith	USC	1940
Linebacker	Les Richter	California	1951
Linebacker	Erny Pinckert	USC	1930-32
Cornerback	Leroy Keyes	Purdue	1967
Cornerback	Jack Tatum	Ohio State	1969-71
Safety	Bob Stiles	UCLA	1966

ALL-TIME PACIFIC COAST CONFERENCE TEAM

Selected in 1948 by vote of the sports editors of the major newspapers in the Pacific Coast Conference area.

First Team

End	Harold (Brick) Muller	California
End	Ted Shipkey	Stanford
Tackle	Glenn (Turk) Edwards	Washington State
Tackle	Ernie Smith	USC
Guard	Bill Corbus	Stanford
Guard	Aaron Rosenberg	USC
Center	Mel Hein	Washington State
Back	George Wilson	Washington
Back	Ernie Nevers	Stanford
Back	Morley Drury	USC
Back	Kenny Washington	UCLA

Second Team

End	James (Monk) Moscrip	Stanford
End	Keith Topping	Stanford
Tackle	Bob Reynolds	Stanford
Tackle	Raymond (Tay) Brown	USC
Guard	Johnny Baker	USC
Guard	Seraphim Post	Stanford
Center	Edwin (Babe) Horrell	California
Back	Frankie Albert	Stanford
Back	Erny Pinckert	USC
Back	Vic Bottari	California
Back	Shy Huntington	Oregon

Third Team

End	Bill Smith	Washington
End	Morris (Red) Badgro	USC
Tackle	Paul Schwegler	Washington
Tackle	Johnny Beckett	Oregon
Guard	Larry Stevens	USC
Guard	Eberle Schultz	Oregon State
Center	Bob Herwig	California
Back	Bobby Grayson	Stanford
Back	Johnny Kitzmiller	Oregon
Back	Norman (Red) Franklin	Oregon State
Back	Gaius (Gus) Shaver	USC

ALL-TIME PACIFIC COAST TEAM 1920-1969

To help celebrate the centennial of college football in 1969, a panel of West Coast newspapermen picked this lineup to represent the Pacifc Coast.

Center	Mel Hein	Washington State	1928-30
Guard	Aaron Rosenberg	USC	1931-33
Guard	Les Richter	California	1950-51
Tackle	Bob Reynolds	Stanford	1933-35
Tackle	Bob Reinhard	California	1940-41
End	Harold (Brick) Muller	California	1920-22
End	Francis Tappaan	USC	1927-29
Back	Ernie Nevers	Stanford	1923-25
Back	George Wilson	Washington	1925
Back	Morley Drury	USC	1925-27
Back	O.J. Simpson	USC	1967-68

Honorable mentions from USC: Tackles — Ron Yary, 1965-67; Ernie Smith, 1930-32. Back — Mike Garrett, 1963-65.

O.J. Simpson

Francis Tappaan

TROJAN HEAD FOOTBALL COACHES

Name	W	L	T	Pct.
Henry H. Goddard and Frank H. Suffell, 1888				
	2	0	0	1.000
Lewis R. Freeman, 1897 (Stanford)	5	1	0	.833
Clair S. Tappaan, 1901 (Syracuse)	0	1	1	.000
John Walker, 1903	4	2	0	.667
Harvey R. Holmes, 1904-07 (Wisconsin)	19	5	3	.759
William I. Traeger, 1908 (Stanford)	3	1	1	.700
Dean B. Cromwell, 1909-10, 1916-18 (Occidental)				
	21	8	6	.686
Ralph Glaze, 1914-15 (Dartmouth)	7	7	0	.500
Elmer C. (Gus) Henderson, 1919-24 (Oberlin)				
	45	7	0	.865
Howard H. Jones, 1925-40 (Yale)	121	36	13	.750
Justin M. (Sam) Barry, 1941 (Wisconsin)	2	6	1	.278
Newell J. Cravath, 1942-50 (USC)	54	28	8	.644
Jesse T. (Jess) Hill, 1951-56 (USC)	45	17	1	.722
Don R. Clark, 1957-59 (USC)	13	16	1	.450
John McKay, 1960-75 (Oregon)	127	40	8	.749
John Robinson, 1976- (Oregon)	50	8	2	.850

Dean Cromwell

Jess Hill

Don Clark

INDIVIDUAL BOWL-GAME HONORS

USC has played in 24 bowl games — 22 Rose, one Liberty and one Bluebonnet. Players of the Game or Most Valuable Players have been picked after each one, and quite often these awards have gone to Trojans. USC is famous for its tailbacks, but note the number of quarterback winners. (The game referred to is the Rose Bowl unless otherwise noted.)

1923	Leo Calland, G
1930	Russ Saunders, QB
1932	Homer Griffith, QB
1939	Doyle Nave, QB
	Al Krueger, E
1940	Ambrose Schindler, QB
1944	Norman Verry, G
1945	Jim Hardy, QB
1953	Rudy Bukich, QB
1963	Pete Beathard, QB
1968	O.J. Simpson, TB
1970	Bob Chandler, FL
1973	Sam Cunningham, FB
1975	Pat Haden, QB
	J.K. McKay, SE
1975	Ricky Bell, TB (Liberty Bowl)
1977	Vince Evans, QB
1977	Rob Hertel, QB (offense) (Bluebonnet Bowl)
	Walt Underwood, DT (defense)
1979	Charles White, TB (co-winner with Michigan QB Rick Leach)
1980	Charles White, TB

Bob Chandler

Rob Hertel

J.K. McKay

Walt Underwood

USC VOIT TROPHY WINNERS

This annual award went to the outstanding football player on the Pacific Coast, as selected by a vote of reporters. The first winner was Stanford's Bill McColl in 1951. The sporting-goods company stopped giving the award after 1978.

1952	Jim Sears
1955	Jon Arnett
1956	Jon Arnett
1965	Mike Garrett
1968	O.J. Simpson
1972	Anthony Davis
1974	Anthony Davis
1976	Ricky Bell
1978	Charles White (shared with UCLA's Jerry Robinson)

USC-NOTRE DAME PLAYERS OF THE GAME

In the 1960s, sports writer/sportscaster Bud Furillo and W.R. (Bill) Schroeder, director of the Citizens Savings Athletic Foundation (formerly Helms Athletic Foundation), retroactively picked the players of the game. The lists appeared in the Coliseum programs. Schroeder updated the selections for this book.

1926	Art Parisien	Notre Dame
1927	Morley Drury	USC
1928	Russ Saunders	USC
1929	Frank Carideo	Notre Dame
1930	Bucky O'Conner	Notre Dame
1931	Johnny Baker	USC
1932	Ernie Smith	USC
1933	Irvine (Cotton) Warburton	USC
1934	Mike Layden	Notre Dame
1935	Bill Shakespeare	Notre Dame
1936	Lawrence (Bud) Langley	USC
1937	Harry Smith	USC
1938	Ollie Day	USC
1939	Ambrose Schindler	USC
1940	Milt Piepul	Notre Dame
1941	Bob Musick	USC
1942	Angelo Bertelli	Notre Dame
1943-45	(no games)	
1946	Johnny Lujack	Notre Dame
1947	George Conner	Notre Dame
1948	Bill Martin	USC
1949	Leon Hart	Notre Dame
1950	Jim Sears	USC
1951	Ralph Guglielmi	Notre Dame
1952	John Lattner	Notre Dame
1953	John Lattner	Notre Dame
1954	Jim Morse	Notre Dame
1955	Jon Arnett	USC
1956	Paul Hornung	Notre Dame
1957	Gerry Gray	Notre Dame
1958	Don Buford	USC
1959	Monty Stickles	Notre Dame
1960	Daryle Lamonica	Notre Dame
1961	Nick Buoniconti	Notre Dame
1962	Ben Wilson	USC
1963	Tommy McDonald	Notre Dame
1964	Craig Fertig	USC
1965	Larry Conjar	Notre Dame
1966	Coley O'Brien	Notre Dame
1967	O.J. Simpson	USC
1968	Joe Theismann	Notre Dame
1969	Al Cowlings	USC
1970	Jimmy Jones	USC
	Joe Theismann	Notre Dame
1971	Edesel Garrison	USC
1972	Anthony Davis	USC
1973	Eric Penick	Notre Dame
1974	Anthony Davis	USC
1975	Ricky Bell	USC
1976	Randy Simmrin	USC
1977	Ken MacAfee	Notre Dame
	Joe Montana	Notre Dame
1978	Paul McDonald	USC
	Charles White	USC
1979	Paul McDonald	USC
	Charles White	USC
1980	William (Chip) Banks	USC

Craig Fertig

TROJANS IN PRO FOOTBALL HALL OF FAME

Class	Player, Position	Teams
1977	Frank Gifford, HB	New York Giants
1979	Ron Mix, T	San Diego Chargers, Oakland Raiders
1981	Morris (Red) Badgro, E	New York Yankees, New York Giants, Brooklyn Dodgers

Three former USC football players have ben inducted into the museum in Canton, Ohio. Morris (Red) Badgro had to wait 45 years after his last game with the 1936 Brooklyn Dodgers to be named, and is the oldest living man to be selected to the Hall. However, Willie Wood, six times an All-Pro defensive back with the Green Bay Packers, and O.J. Simpson, five-time All-Pro running back for Buffalo and San Francisco are candidates.

Frank Gifford   Ron Mix

Morris (Red) Badgro

CHICAGO COLLEGE ALL-STAR GAME STARTERS

The College All-Star Game was begun in 1934, featuring selected college graduating seniors versus the Chicago Bears, who had won the National Football League title in 1933. Following are Trojans who were named as starters during the series, which was discontinued after 1976.

1934	Homer Griffith, QB
1940	Bill Fisk, LE
	Harry Smith, RG
	Ambrose Schindler, QB
	(ran for two touchdowns)
1946	Ralph Heywood, RE
1948	Paul Cleary, LE
1953	Jim Sears, RH
1957	Jon Arnett, LH
1962	Frank Buncom, LB
1964	Pete Beathard, QB
1968	Ron Yary, T
	Adrian Young, LB
1969	Bob Klein, TC
1970	Sid Smith, C
	Al Cowlings, DE
1971	Marv Montgomery, T
1972	Willie Hall, LB
1973	John McKay, All-Stars Head Coach
	Pete Adams, T
	Dave Brown, C
	Charles Young, TE
	John Grant, DT
1975	John McKay, All-Stars Head Coach
	Richard Wood, LB
	Charles Phillips, S
	Marvin Cobb, S

Bob Klein   Al Cowlings   Sid Smith   Willie Hall

Marlin McKeever

NFL FIRST-ROUND DRAFT PICKS

1940	Grenny Landsdell, B	New York Giants
1940	Doyle Nave, B	Detroit Lions
1942	Bob Robertson, B	Brooklyn Dodgers
1945	Jim Hardy, QB	Washington Redskins
1946	Leo Riggs, B*	Philadelphia Eagles
1952	Frank Gifford, B	New York Giants
1953	Al Carmichael, B	Green Bay Packers
1957	Jon Arnett, RB	Los Angeles Rams
1960	Ron Mix, T	Baltimore Colts
1961	Marlin McKeever, E-LB	Los Angeles Rams
1964	Pete Beathard, QB	Detroit Lions and Kansas City Chiefs (then in rival leagues)
1968	Mike Hull, RB	Chicago Bears
1968	Tim Rossovich, DE	Philadelphia Eagles
1968	Mike Taylor, T	Pittsburgh Steelers
1968	Ron Yary, T	Minnesota Vikings
1969	Bob Klein, TE	Los Angeles Rams
1969	O.J. Simpson, RB	Buffalo Bills
1970	Al Cowlings, DE	Buffalo Bills
1970	Sid Smith, T	Kansas City Chiefs
1971	Marv Montgomery, T	Denver Broncos
1971	Tody Smith, DE	Dallas Cowboys
1973	Pete Adams, T	Cleveland Browns
1974	Lynn Swann, WR	Pittsburgh Steelers
1975	Bill Bain, G†	Green Bay Packers
1975	Anthony Davis, RB†	New York Jets
1977	Ricky Bell, RB	Tampa Bay Buccaneers
1977	Gary Jeter, DT	New York Giants
1977	Marvin Powell, T	New York Jets
1978	Clay Matthews, LB	Cleveland Browns
1980	Brad Budde, G	Kansas City Chiefs
1980	Anthony Munoz, T	Cincinnati Bengals
1980	Charles White, RB	Cleveland Browns
1981	Ronnie Lott, S	San Francisco 49ers
1981	Dennis Smith, S	Denver Broncos
1981	Keith Van Horne, T	Chicago Bears

*Riggs came out of Bell High School and played on the 1942 freshman team with tackle John Ferraro, also from Bell. He was a great varsity prospect. However, when he came back after three years at sea in World War II, he wasn't the same player. He did not letter at USC and did not play pro ball.

†Bain and Davis were the first picks of the Packers and Jets respectively, but those picks came on the second round because the clubs had traded away their first-round choices.

Jon Arnett

Clay Matthews

Marv Montgomery

Dennis Smith

John Robinson and 1980 NFL first round selections Charles White, Brad Budde, and Anthony Munoz.

TROJANS WHO HAVE MADE ALL-PRO

1931	Morris (Red) Badgro, E	New York Giants
1932	Nate Barragar, C	Green Bay Packers
1933	Morris (Red) Badgro, E	New York Giants
1934	Morris (Red) Badgro, E	New York Giants
1936	Ernie Smith, T	Green Bay Packers
1955	Frank Gifford, HB	New York Giants
1956	Charley Ane, C	Detroit Lions
	Frank Gifford, HB	New York Giants
1957	Frank Gifford, HB	New York Giants
1958	Jon Arnett, HB	Los Angeles Rams
1959	Frank Gifford, HB	New York Giants
1960 (AFL)	Ron Mix, T*	Los Angeles Chargers
	Volney Peters, DT	Los Angeles Chargers
1961 (AFL)	Ron Mix, T	San Diego Chargers
1962 (AFL)	Ron Mix, T	San Diego Chargers
1963 (NFL)	Willie Wood, S	Green Bay Packers
(AFL)	Ron Mix, T	San Diego Chargers
1964 (NFL)	Willie Wood, S	Green Bay Packers
(AFL)	Ron Mix, T	San Diego Chargers
1965 (NFL)	Willie Wood, S	Green Bay Packers
1966 (NFL)	Willie Wood, S	Green Bay Packers
1967 (NFL)	Willie Wood, S	Green Bay Packers
(AFL)	Ron Mix, T	San Diego Chargers
	Mike Garrett, RB	Kansas City Chiefs
1968 (NFL)	Willie Wood, S	Green Bay Packers
(AFL)	Ron Mix, T	San Diego Chargers
1971	Ron Yary, T	Minnesota Vikings
1972	O.J. Simpson, RB	Buffalo Bills
1973	Charles Young, TE	Philadelphia Eagles
	Ron Yary, T	Minnesota Vikings
	O.J. Simpson, RB	Buffalo Bills
1974	Ron Yary, T	Minnesota Vikings
	O.J. Simpson, RB	Buffalo Bills
1975	Lynn Swann, WR	Pittsburgh Steelers
	Charles Young, TE	Philadelphia Eagles
	Ron Yary, T	Minnesota Vikings
	O.J. Simpson, RB	Buffalo Bills
1976	Ron Yary, T	Minnesota Vikings
	O.J. Simpson, RB	Buffalo Bills
1978	Lynn Swann, WR	Pittsburgh Steelers
1979	Marvin Powell, T	New York Jets
1980	Marvin Powell, T	New York Jets

*Picked for the All-Time AFL team by a Pro Football Hall of Fame committee

CAPTAINS

Year	Captain	Year	Captain
1888	Will Whitcomb	1936	Gil Kuhn
1889	No Captain	1937	Chuck Williams
1890	No Varsity	1938	Don McNeil
1891	Frank Lapham	1939	Joe Shell
1892	No Varsity	1940	Ed Dempsey
1893	No Captain	1941	Bob de Lauer
1894	John A. Gray	1942	Don Willer
1895	Lee Bradley	1943	Ralph Heywood
1896	Foster Wright	1944	Jim Hardy
1897	Harry Martin	1945	Jim Callanan
1898	Foster Wright	1946	Doug Essick
1899	Logan Wheatley	1947	Don Clark
1900	Harry Woodard	1948	Bob Bastian
1901	Logan Wheatley	1949	Jim Bird
1902	Daril Caley	1950	Paul McMurtry, Volney Peters
1903	Daril Caley	1951	Pat Cannamela, Dean Schneider
1904	Jay Bickford	1952	Bob Van Doren, Lou Welsh
1905	Carl Elliott	1953	George Bozanic, Tom Nickoloff
1906	Oliver Best	1954	Ed Fouch, Lindon Crow
1907	Charley Haigler	1955	George Galli, Marv Goux
1908	Stan Burek	1956	Jon Arnett, Ellsworth Kissinger
1909	Hal Paulin	1957	Jim Conroy, Mike Henry
1910	Jack Malcolm	1958	Ken Antle, Monte Clark
1911–13	Rugby	1959	Ron Mix, Willie Wood
1914	Tommy Davis	1960	Mike McKeever, George Van Vliet
1915	Len Livernash	1961	Britt Williams
1916	Herb Jones	1962	Marv Marinovich, Ben Wilson
1917	Frank Malette	1963	Pete Beathard, Willie Brown
1918	Harold Galloway, Keith Hunter	1964	Craig Fertig, Bill Fisk, Jr.
1919	John Fox	1965	Chuck Arrobio, Mike Garrett
1920	Roy Evans	1966	Nate Shaw, Rod Sherman
1921	Charley Dean	1967	Tim Rossovich, Adrian Young
1922	Leo Calland	1968	O.J. Simpson, Steve Sogge
1923	Chet Dolley	1969	Jim Gunn, Bob Jensen
1924	John Hawkins	1970	Charlie Weaver, Bob Chandler
1925	Hobbs Adams	1971	John Vella, Willie Hall
1926	Newell (Jeff) Cravath	1972	Sam Cunningham, John Grant
1927	Morley Drury	1973	Lynn Swann, Artimus Parker
1928	Jesse Hibbs	1974	Pat Haden, Richard Wood
1929	Nate Barragar	1975	Kevin Bruce, Danny Reece
1930	Marshall Duffield	1976	Ricky Bell, Vince Evans
1931	Stan Williamson		Eric Williams
1932	Raymond (Tay) Brown	1977	Rob Hertel, Clay Matthews
1933	Ford Palmer	1978	Lynn Cain, Rich Dimler
1934	Julie Bescos	1979	Dennis Johnson, Charles White
1935	Art Dittberner, Cliff Propst	1980	Ronnie Lott, Keith Van Horne

FOOTBALL PLAYERS WHO PARTICIPATED IN OTHER SPORTS

Baseball
Hobbs Adams
Rob Adolph
Charles Ane
Joe Austin
Morris (Red) Badgro
Julie Bescos
Willie Brown
Don Buford
Marvin Cobb
Anthony Davis
Walt Failor
Mike Garrett
Ed Gilliam
Jim Hardy
Rob Hertel
Fred Hill
Jess Hill
Ray Ingle
Ed Isherwood
Rex Johnston
Manuel Laraneta
Bob Levingston
Orv Mohler
Anthony Munoz
Paul Salata
Steve Sogge
Fay Thomas
Bob Winslow
Ernie Zampese

Basketball
Morris (Red) Badgro
Julie Bescos
Morley Drury
Manuel Laraneta
Jess Mortensen
Roderick Thompson

Golf
Bob Lee

Gymnastics
Bob Hoffman

Ice Hockey
Morley Drury
Bob Hoffman

Track & Field
Jon Arnett
Al Barry
Jim Bates
Wilson Bowie
Dick Bronson
Ken Carpenter
Allen Carter
Bob Chandler
Leon Clarke
Angelo Coia
Rod Connors
Jim Decker
Robert A. (Buck) Fisher
Herman Franklin
Edesel Garrison
Owen Hansen
Luther Hayes
Jess Hill
Ed Johnson
Mort Kaer
Fred Kelly
Desmond Koch
Jim Lawrence
Eddie Leahy
Bob Lee
Phil Lee
Steve Lehmer
Earl McCullouch
Marlin McKeever
Mike McKeever
Don McNeil
Jess Mortensen*
Mike Page
Ken Randle
C.R. Roberts
Rod Sherman
O.J. Simpson
Dennis Smith
Bruce Taylor
Theo Viltz
Bob Voiles
Elmer Willhoite
Kevin Williams

Volleyball
Steve Obradovich

Water Polo
Morley Drury

*National decathlon champ, as well as an All-America in basketball.

Morris (Red) Badgro

Orv Mohler

Jess Mortensen

Steve Sogge

Fred Hill

Earl McCullouch

Steve Lehmer

Kevin Williams

Anthony Munoz

FOOTBALL PLAYERS WHO MADE IT IN SHOW BIZ

Ward Bond — Letterman of 1928-29-30 was best known for his starring role in the TV series *Wagon Train*, but for many years before that he was a busy supporting actor. His films included *The Informer* (1935), *Tobacco Road* (1941), *The Quiet Man* (1952), and *The Searchers* (1956). He died in 1960.

Frank Gifford — His acting career amounted to little despite his good looks. A longtime sportscaster for the ABC-TV network, Gifford is frequently seen in television and magazine advertisements.

Mike Henry — After a good pro football career playing for the Steelers and the Rams, he turned to acting and was one of the many ex-athletes who played the role of Tarzan.

Jesse Hibbs — A two-time All-America tackle, he became a successful movie and TV director. Some of his films: *All American* (1953), *Black Horse Canyon* (1955), *Ride a Crooked Trail* (1958).

Ron Miller — An end in the early 1950s, he is now the president and chief executive officer of Walt Disney Productions.

Aaron Rosenberg — All-America lineman in the early 1930s. Before his death in 1979, he produced 70 movies, including the Marlon Brando version of *Mutiny on the Bounty* and *Winchester 73*.

Eddie Saenz — Film and TV stunt man.

O.J. Simpson — Not only is "Juice" big in commercials for Hertz and other corporations, but he has had several starring roles in movies, including the recent made-for-TV feature, *Goldie and the Boxer*.

Irvine (Cotton) Warburton — The 1933 All-America back was one of Hollywood's most respected film editors until his recent retirement. He won an Oscar for editing the Walt Disney film *Mary Poppins*.

John Wayne — He was Marion Morrison when he was in the Sigma Chi house at USC and playing for Howard Jones. However, he left school to pursue an acting career and, unlike his pal Ward Bond, never lettered. Some of his greatest movies: *Stagecoach* (1939), *Red River* (1948), *The Quiet Man* (1952), and *True Grit* (1969), for which he won an Oscar.

OTHER NCAA TEAMS NICKNAMED TROJANS

Greek names are not nearly as popular as Wildcats, Rams, Bears, Tigers, Eagles, and the ferocious like, but there are five Spartans (and one Thundering Herd — Marshall U. in Huntington, West Virginia). Besides USC there are only three other Trojans:

Arkansas-Little Rock	Little Rock, Arkansas
Troy State	Troy, Alabama
Virginia State	Petersburg, Virginia

Marion M. Morrison (John Wayne)

Jesse Hibbs

Ron Miller

FOOTBALL LETTERMEN WHO PLAYED MAJOR-LEAGUE BASEBALL

Morris (Red) Badgro — A fine end for the Trojans in the mid-'20s, the Washington native was All-Pro for the New York Giants and was inducted into the Pro Football Hall of Fame in 1981. He was an outfielder two seasons with the old St. Louis Browns, 1929 and 1930, and hit .284 in 54 games in 1929.

Don Buford — USC's rushing leader in 1958 became a regular for the Chicago White Sox and Baltimore Orioles. He played both infield and outfield and hit .264 in 10 seasons.

Jess Hill — One of USC's greatest all-around athletes, Hill was a substitute fullback for Howard Jones. He hit .293 in 107 games with the New York Yankees in 1935. His four-year American League batting average: .289.

Rex Johnston — A starting halfback in the late 1950s, his baseball career didn't amount to much: seven at-bats with the Pittsburgh Pirates in 1964, no hits.

Fay Thomas — A football letterman in 1923 and 1924, he pitched 81 games for four different teams in the big leagues. Lifetime record: 9-20.

Morris (Red) Badgro   *Don Buford*

Traveler II

TOP FIVE STUDENT-ATHLETES

Candidates for the NCAA's Today's Top Five Student-Athlete awards are selected for their "athletic ability, achievement, character, leadership, campus and off-campus activities, and academic achievement." USC has had five winners since the program started in 1972, three of them from football. Three other Trojan football players were finalists.

1972	Dave Brown (one of 15 finalists)	
1973	Monte Doris (one of 15 finalists)	
1974	Pat Haden	
1975	Marvin Cobb	
1979	Paul McDonald	
1980	Keith Van Horne	
	(one of five fall finalists)	

Dave Brown   *Monte Doris*

Marvin Cobb   *Keith Van Horne*

NCAA POSTGRADUATE SCHOLARSHIPS

Through 1980, USC had won more NCAA postgraduate scholarships than any other school (25), ahead of the Air Force Academy (22), Stanford (21), Notre Dame (20), and Dartmouth (18). Here are the Trojan football players who have won:

1965	Chuck Arrobio	1974	Marvin Cobb
1968	Steve Sogge	1975	Kevin Bruce
1969	Fred Khasigian	1977	Gary Bethel
1969	Steve Lehmer	1979	Brad Budde
1973	Monte Doris	1979	Paul McDonald
1974	Pat Haden*	1980	Gordon Adams

*Also a Rhodes Scholar.

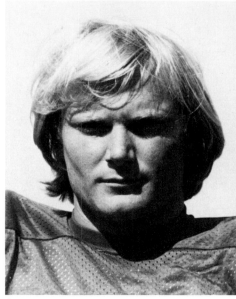

Pat Haden

BROTHERS

Jon Arnett	1954-55-56
Bob Arnett	1957-58
Richard Berryman	1936
Robert Berryman	1939-40
Bill Bledsoe	1940-41
Leo Bledsoe	1941
Joey Browner	1979-80
Keith Browner	1980
Louis Byrd	1957-58
MacArthur Byrd	1962-63-64
Howard Callanan	1942
George Callanan	1943
Jim Callanan	1944-45-46
John Dye	1931-32-33
William Dye	1933-34
John Fouch	1949-50
Ed Fouch	1952-53-54
Ron Gallaher	1969-70
Allen Gallaher	1970-71-72
Ben Gerpheide	1923
Louis Gerpheide	1923
Chester Haigler	1905-06
Charles Haigler	1905-06-07-08
Don Hardy	1942-43-44
Jim Hardy	1942-42-44
Jerry Hayhoe	1964-66
Bill Hayhoe	1967-68
Jesse Hibbs	1926-27-28
Gene Hibbs	1935-36-37
Bob Hooks	1951-52
Roger Hooks	1954
Jim Jones	1936-37-38
Bob Jones	1939-40-41
Logan Lindley	1918-19-20-21
Lowell Lindley	1920-21-22
Dick Manning	1941
Travis Manning	Did not letter
Clay Matthews	1974-75-76-77
Bruce Matthews	1980
Marlin McKeever	1958-59-60
Mike McKeever	1958-59-60
Bob McNeish	1931-32-33
George McNeish	1934-35-36
Manfred Moore	1971-72-73
Kenney Moore	1978-79-80
Malcolm Moore	1980
James Musick	1929-30-31
Bill Musick	1941
Bob Musick	1941-42-45
John (Jack) Musick	1944-45-46
Johnny Naumu	1946
Sol Naumu	1950
Jim Obradovich	1973-74
Steve Obradovich	1976
Ralph Pucci	1948-49-50
Ed Pucci	1951-52-53
John Seixas	1932-33
Bill Seixas	1942
Bob Stillwell	1947-48-49
Don Stillwell	1950-51-52
Troy Winslow	1965-66
Gary Winslow	Did not letter
Ray Woods	1940-41-42
Roy Woods	Did not letter
John Vella	1969-70-71
Chris Vella	1971-72
Ron Yary	1965-66-67
Wayne Yary	1969-70

FATHERS AND SONS

Bill Fisk*	1937-38-39
Bill Fisk, Jr.	1962-63-64
Ray George*	1936-37-38
Greg George	Did not letter
Ted (Butter) Gorrell	1924-25-26
Walt Gorrell	1956
Bruce Hull	1934-35
Mike Hull	1965-66-67
Charles Page	Head Coach, 1960-75
J.K. McKay	1972-73-74
Chuck Page	1943
Toby Page	1966-67
Bob Winslow*	1937-38-39
Troy Winslow	1965-66
Gary Winslow	Did not letter

*Also served as an assistant football coach at USC.

TRANSFERS

Many Trojan football players went to USC after playing at and/or attending junior colleges. The list includes Frank Gifford, O.J. Simpson, Damon Bame, Ron Yary, Mike Battle, Jess Hill, Marv Goux, Ray May, Hal Bedsole and Jim Sears. But a few transferred from other universities. Here are some of the more prominent ones:

Roy (Bullet) Baker	Santa Clara
Rudy Bukich	Iowa
Mike Garzoni	Fresno State
"Speedy" Hart	Notre Dame
Frank Jordan	UC Riverside
Ted Ossowski	Oregon State
Vic Rakhshani	San Jose State
Eddie Saenz	Loyola (L.A.)
Bob Schmidt	Notre Dame
Rod Sherman	UCLA
Tody Smith	Michigan State
Calvin Sweeney	UC Riverside
Jack Willis	Tennessee

Roy (Bullet) Baker   *Tody Smith*

NICKNAMES

Antelope Al	Al Krueger
B-Boys	Pete Beathard, Hal Bedsole, Willie Brown, Ben Wilson
Bambi	Mike Hull
Blackjack	Harry Smith
Bug	Kevin Williams (5-9, 165)
Bullet	Roy Baker
Butter	Ted Gorrell
Cardiac Kids	1968 and 1969 teams
Cotton	Irvine Warburton
The Duck	Mike Garrett
End Around	Ray Sparling
Field Marshall	Marshall Duffield
Gloomy Gus	Coach Elmer Henderson
Hobo	Howard Kincaid
Iron Mike	Mike Garrett
Jaguar Jon	Jon Arnett
Juice	O.J. Simpson
The Noblest Trojan of Them All	Morley Drury
Prince Hal	Hal Bedsole
Racehorse	Russell Saunders
Sam Bam	Sam Cunningham
Sugarbear	Charles Hinton
The Thundering Herd	Howard Jones' teams
Tree	Charles Young (6-4, 228)
The Wild Bunch	1969 defensive line led by Al Cowlings, Jimmy Gunn, Tody Smith, and Charlie Weaver.

ALL-TIME ROSTER OF LETTER WINNERS

Various standards have been used to determine USC letter winners over the years, but since 1976 squad members who have played at least 30 minutes have been listed as lettermen. There have been many exceptions to that rule, including kickers and others who contributed significantly to the team's success without playing 30 minutes. In addition, senior squad members have generally been awarded letters for their senior seasons, as long as they appeared in at least one game.

A

Abram, Fabian 1955–56
Achica, George 1979–80
Acker, Frank 1904–05
Adams, Gene 1904–05
Adams, Gordon 1980
Adams, Halley 1922–23–24
Adams, Harold 1923–24–25
Adams, Peter 1970–71–72
Adams, William J. 1967
Adelman, Harry 1941–42
Adolph, Robyn 1973–74
Aguirre, John 1941–45
Aldridge, Charles 1967
Aleksi, Joe 1925–27
Alexander, Harold 1923
Allan, Roy 1908–09–10
Allen, Marcus 1978–79–80
Allmon, Richard C. 1967–68
Almy, J. 1907
Anderson, Charles A. 1960–61
Anderson, Norman 1922–23–24
Anderson, Otto 1922–23–24
Anderson, William C. 1937–38–39–40
Ane, Charles T., Jr. 1951–52
Anthony, Charles 1971–72–73
Anthony, Frank 1927–28–29
Antle, Ken Lee 1956–57–58
Antles, Russell 1944–45–46
Apsit, Marger 1928–29–30
Arbelbide, Garrett 1929–30–31
Arnest, Henry C. 1961
Arnett, Bob 1957–58
Arnett, Jon 1954–55–56
Arnold, James 1918
Arnold, Paul 1889
Arrobio, Charles Augustus 1963–64–65
Artenian, Mickey 1952–53
Ashcraft, Walt 1949–52
Atanasoff, Alex 1937
Audet, Earl 1943
Avery, Ralph 1896–97
Axe, Fred 1919–20–21
Ayala, Victor Ronald 1968–69–70

B

Baccitich, John M. 1966
Badgro, Morris 1924–25–26
Bailie, Bert 1904
Bain, Marvin J. 1964–65
Bain, William E. 1973–74
Baker, John 1929–30–31
Baker, Roy 1922–23
Baker, Sam
Baldock, Alvin 1949–50–53
Baldridge, Lyle 1925–26–28
Baley, Burt 1903–05
Bame, Damon 1962–63
Banks, Chip 1978–79–80
Bansavage, Albert A. 1959
Banta, Jack 1938–39–40
Barber, Richard 1931–32
Bardin, Oliver 1932–33
Barnes, Mercer 1949–50
Barragar, Nathan 1927–28–29
Barrager 1918
Barrett 1917
Barry, Allan 1952
Barry, Nelson 1930
Barry, Stephen Anthony 1965—66
Bastian, Bob 1946—47—48
Bates, James Edward 1960—61
Battle, Art 1946–48–49
Battle, Michael 1966–67–68
Bayley, Eugene 1914
Beale, John Paul 1918–19–20
Beals 1917
Beard, Francis 1932–33–34
Beard, Gregory S. 1975
Beathard, Peter 1961–62–63
Beattie, Eugene 1926–27

Beatty, Blanchard 1930–31
Beatty, Homer 1934–35–36
Beck, Eugene 1948–49–50
Becker, Henry 1929
Bedsole, Harold J. 1961–62–63
Beeson, Bob 1940
Behrendt, Allen 1924–25–26
Belko, Max 1934–35–36
Bell, Howard 1926
Bell, Joseph A. 1943
Bell, Ricky L. 1973–74–75–76
Belotti, D. George 1954–55–56
Bennett, Frank 1939
Benson, Carl 1939–40
Berry, Michael H. 1969–70
Berryman, Richard 1936
Berryman, Robert 1939–40
Bescos, Julius 1932–33–34
Best, Oliver 1904
Bethel, Gary W. 1975–76–77
Bettinger, George 1935
Betz, Bill 1947
Bianchi, Steve 1941
Bickford, John H. 1903–04–06
Biggs, Henry 1930–31–32
Bird, Jim 1947–48–49
Bird, Richard 1919–20
Black, Rupert 1930
Blair, Horace 1922
Blake, Samuel R. 1916
Blanche, John G. 1966–68
Blecksmith, Edward L. 1964–65
Bledsoe, Leo 1941
Bledsoe, William 1940–41
Bleeker, Melvin 1940–41–42
Bockman 1905
Bohlinger, Tom 1972–73
Boice, Winchell 1922
Boies, Herbert 1949
Boies, Larry Kenton 1957–58
Bond, Ward 1928–29–30
Bonham, Herschel 1926–27–28
Bordier, Warner 1954–55
Boren, Charles F. 1925–27–28
Born, Dennis L. 1967
Bosbyshell, W. 1906
Botelho, Rod 1958
Bott, Clyde 1896–97
Boulware, Dave 1971–72–73
Bowers, William 1950
Bowie, Wilson 1968
Bowman, Charles 1939
Boyle, Johnny 1920–21–22
Bozanic, George 1951–52–53
Bradford, Joe 1945
Bradley, Joe 1895
Bradley, Otha M. 1973–74
Brandt, Harvey T. 1934
Braziel, Larry 1977–78
Brenner, Hoby 1978–79–80
Bridewell, Walter 1907
Bright, Kenneth 1932–33
Brockman, Kenneth 1919
Broderson, Charles 1898–1902–03–04
Brooks, Bruce 1977
Bronson, Richard 1957
Brouse, Willard 1931
Brousseau, Raphael 1935–36–37
Brown, Booker 1972–73
Brown, David 1970–71–72
Brown, Everett 1928–29–30
Brown, F.R. 1906–08
Brown, George E. 1934
Brown, George L. 1889
Brown, Jeff 1980
Brown, Raymond (Tay) 1930–31–32
Brown, Ronald Lee 1954–55
Brown, Willie F. 1961–62–63
Browner, Joey 1979–80
Browner, Keith 1980
Brownell, Richard L. 1964
Browning, Ward 1932–33–34
Brownwood, John R. 1962–63–64
Bruce, Kevin 1973–74–75
Buckley, Robert 1952–53
Budde, Brad 1976–77–78–79
Buford, Don 1957–58
Bukich, Rudy 1951–52
Buncom, Frank 1960–61
Bundra, Mike P. 1959–60–61
Bundy, Bill 1939–40–41
Bunker, Frank 1907–09
Burchard, Gerald 1933–34–35
Burek, Stanley 1905–06–07–08
Burke, Don 1948
Burkett 1916
Burnett, C.W. 1893–95
Burnside, Donald (see Doll)
Burns, Dan 1976–77
Burns, Michael 1975–76
Busby, Marvin L. 1934
Busby, Stuart H. 1961

Busch, Ernie 1947
Busick, Steve 1978–79–80
Bush, Ronald L. 1974–75–76
Butcher, Ronald W. 1961–62
Butler, Raymond 1978–79
Butterfield, Clarence 1917–19–20
Byrd, Glenn 1972
Byrd, MacArthur 1962–63–64
Byrd, Louis 1957–58

C

Cahill, Ray 1966
Cain, Lynn 1977–78
Calabria, Ronald D. 1954
Caley, Daril 1902–03
Caley, Elwyn 1902–03
Callanan, George P. 1943
Callanan, Howard 1942
Callanan, James F. 1944–45–46
Calland, Leo 1920–21–22
Cameron, Don 1923
Cameron, Rodney 1933–34–35
Campbell, Gordon 1921–22–23
Campbell, Jack 1978
Campbell, Jim 1917
Cannamela, Pat 1950–51
Cantor, Al 1948
Cantwell, John T. 1974
Carey, Mike 1976–77
Carmichael, Al 1950–51–52
Carmichael, E. W. 1906
Carpenter, Kenneth 1934–37
Carpenter, Roy 1905–06
Carten, Red 1893
Carter, Allen 1972–73–74
Carter, Kent 1970–71
Carver, C.E. 1889
Case, Frank 1905
Cashman, Patrick F. 1966–67
Cassell, Curtis 1920–21
Catoe, Ed 1976–77
Celotto, Mario 1974–75–76–77
Chambers, Mahlon 1927–28–29
Chandler, Robert D. 1968–69–70
Chaney, Chris 1972
Chantilles, Tom 1941
Charles, Ben F. 1959–60
Chestnut, Bob 1917–19
Christianson 1919
Christie, Charles 1896–97
Chuha, Joe 1957
Clark 1916–17
Clark, Don 1942–46–47
Clark, Gordon 1931–32–33
Clark, Jack 1935
Clark, Jay 1962–63
Clark, Monte Dale 1956–57–58
Clark, Roger A. 1960
Clark, Roger Alan 1961
Clark, Stephen 1905–06–07–08
Clarke, Eugene 1930–31
Clarke, Leon T. 1953–54–55
Clayton, Franklin D. 1952–53–54
Cleary, Paul 1945–46–47
Clemens, Calvin Jr. 1932–33–34
Clemens, Jerry 1919
Cobb, Garry 1976–77–78
Cobb, Marvin L. 1972–73–74
Cochran, C.N. 1909
Coffman, Theadore 1923–24–25
Cohn, Thomas 1910
Coia, Angelo 1958–59
Cole, Ralph W. 1921–24
Colley, Tom 1948
Collins, Pat 1973
Coloneus 1907–08–09
Conde, John 1949–50–51
Connors, Rod 1977
Conroy, James 1956–57–59
Conroy, Jerome G. 1965
Contratto, Jim A. 1953–54–55
Cook, Andrew J. 1924–25
Coones, Ken 1959
Cordell, Michael 1973–74–75
Coughlin, Alvie 1932–33–34
Courdis 1919
Covington, Humphrey L. 1968–69
Cowlings, Allen G. 1968–69
Cox, Kenneth 1924–25–26
Cox, Morgan 1918–19–20
Cox, Robert 1951–52
Coyle, Leslie 1927
Craig, Gerald 1913–14–15–16
Crall 1907
Cramer, Stanley 1947
Crane, Dennis W. 1967
Cravath, Jeff 1924–25–26
Crawford, Willie 1977–78
Crisp 1919
Crittenden, Wallace 1944
Critton 1905

Crow, Lindon 1952–53–54
Crowthers, Jim 1941
Cruickshank, Donald 1924–25–26
Culbreath, Cliff 1972
Cummings, Ralph 1921–22–23
Cunningham, Sam 1970–71–72
Curley, August 1980
Curry, Edsel 1943–46–47
Curry, Willard 1915–16
Curtis, Louis Lane 1944
Custin, George 1906
Cutri, Cosimo 1950–51

D

Dahlgren 1917
Dandoy, Aramis M. 1952–53–54
Danehe, Richard 1941
Darby, Byron 1979–80
DaRe, Mario P. 1952–53–54
Davis, Anthony 1972–73–74
Davis, Clarence E. 1969–70
Davis, David 1934–35–36
Davis, George 1944–47–49
Davis, George 1934
Davis, Joe 1940–41–42
Davis, Joe E. 1973–74–75
Davis, Robert 1922
Davis, Thomas 1911–12–13–14
Day, Oliver 1937–38
Dean Charles F. 1919–20–21
DeArmand 1917
Debovsky, Phillip 1957
Declus, H. 1906–07–09
Decker, George 1929–30
Decker, James Ralph 1953–54–56
DeGroote, Clarke 1924–25–26
Dehetre, John 1934–37
DeKraai, Terry L. 1968–69
Delaney, Gary C. 1960
DeLappe, J.R. 1904
DeLauer, Bob 1939–40–41
Del Conte, Kenneth 1960–61–62
Demirjian, Ed 1960
Dempsey, Edward 1938–39–40
Deranian, Vaughn 1928–29–30
Dickerson, Samuel 1968–69–70
Diehl, Lawrence 1926–27
Diggs, Shelton K. 1973–74–75–76
Dill, Dean 1947
DiLulo, Paul 1978–80
Dimler, Richard A. 1975–76–77–78
Dittberner, Art 1933–34–35
Doll, Don (formerly Burnside) 1944–46–47–48
Dolley, Chet 1922–23–24
Dominis, John 1943
Doris, Monte 1972–73
Dorsey, Gene 1923–24–26
Dougher, Harold 1922
Dougherty, Morton 1902
Douglas, Don 1957–58
Downs, Bob 1950
Drake, Ronald V. 1966–67
Dreblow, Milford 1943–44–45–46
Drury, Morley 1925–26–27
Duboski, Phillip 1936
Duff, Clinton 1949–50–51
Duffield, Marshall 1928–29–30
Dunaway, Warren 1934
Dunn, Coye 1936
Dunning, Corwin 1932
DuPuy, Reginald 1922–23–24
Durkee, Harvey 1928–29–30
Durko, Sandy V. 1968–69
Duvall, Gordon C. 1953–54–55
Dye, George 1929
Dye, John 1931–32–33
Dye, William 1933–34
Dyer, Bruce 1970–71

E

Earle, Raymond 1923–24–25
Edelson, Henry 1927–28–29
Edgarton, E.O. 1896
Edwards, Dennis 1978–79–80
Edwards, Hugh 1925
Edwards, Robert 1958–59
Egan, John G. 1920
Elliott, Carl 1904–05–06
Elliott, E. 1893
Elliott, Earl 1904
Elliott, Howard 1925–26–27
Elliott, Ian 1941
Elmore, John Jr. 1914
Embree, A.B. 1889–92
Emmons, Richard 1922
Engle, Roy 1937–38–39
Enright, Richard M. 1954–55
Eriksen, Bob 1971
Erskine, Robert 1931–32–33

Essick, Douglas 1941–42–43
Evans, R. 1917
Evans, Charles 1969–70
Evans, John 1943
Evans, Roy 1919–20–21
Evans, Vincent T. 1974–75–76
Exley, Landon M. 1952–53

F

Failor, Walt 1970
Farmer, David W. 1974–75–76
Fassell, Jim E. 1969
Fate, Steve 1971–72
Fay, Kenneth 1931–32–33
Ferguson, Claude 1902
Ferguson, James T. 1966
Ferrante, Orlando 1953–54–55
Ferraro, John 1943–44–46–47
Fertig, Craig W. 1962–63–64
Ficca, Dan 1958–59–60
Finneran, Gary 1957–58–59
Finney, Hal 1942
Fiorentino, Frank 1956–57–58
Fisher, Jeff 1979–80
Fisher, Robert A. 1936–37–38
Fisk, Bill 1937–38–39
Fisk, Bill Jr. 1962–63–64
Fite, Gary G. 1965
Fletcher, Oliver 1948
Fletcher, Paul 1905–06
Fletcher, Ronald 1954–55–56
Flint, Ray 1902–03
Flood, Jeff 1973–75
Floro, Robert S. 1960
Follett, George 1971–72
Foote, Chris 1977–78–79
Ford, Dwight W. 1974–75–77–78
Ford, William 1926–28
Foster, Roy 1978–79–80
Fouch, Edward V. 1952–53–54
Fouch, John 1949–50
Fox, Jack 1926–27
Fox, John 1915, 16, 19
Fraser, Scott 1977–79
Freeman, George 1921–22–23
Friend, Bill 1924–25–26
Fuhrer, Bob 1932–33–34
Fuhrman, Seymour 1942
Funk, J.B. 1894

G

Gaisford, Bill 1935–36
Gale, Michael 1961–62
Galindo, Charles 1925
Gallaher, Allen 1970–71–72
Galli, George 1953–54–55
Galloway, Amor 1921–22
Galloway, Clark 1927–28–29
Galloway, Harold 1918–22
Galvin, Glen 1936–37–39
Garcia, Dan 1978–79
Garlin, Donald 1944–46–47–48
Garrett, Michael 1963–64–65
Garrison, Edesel 1971–72
Garzoni, Mike 1943–44–45–46
Gaskill, Lynn 1959–60–61
Gaspar, Phil 1937–38–39
Gay, William H. 1975–76–77
Gee, Doug 1945
Gelker, Benjamin B. 1943
Geller, Roscoe 1908–09
Gentry, Byron 1930-31-32
George, Ray, 1936–37–38
Gerpheide, Ben 1923
Gerpheide, Louis 1923
Getz, Bob 1932
Gibson, Anthony 1980
Giers, Michael L. 1963–64
Gifford, Frank 1949–50–51
Giguette, Al 1904–05
Gill, William J. 1934–35
Givehand, James 1972
Glenn, William 1922
Goller, Winston 1950–51
Gonta, Stanley L. 1962
Goodenow, Harold 1906–07–08
Gordon, Clifford 1920–21
Gorrell, Ted 1924–25–26
Gorrell, Walter T. 1956
Goux, Marvin A. 1952–54–55
Gowder, Robert 1927–28–29
Gracin, Jerry 1934
Grady, Stephen 1966–67
Graf, Allan 1970–71–72
Grant, John 1970–71–72
Gray, Gordon 1943–44–46–47
Gray, John A. 1889–92–93
Gray, Kenneth 1972–73–74
Gray, Riki 1978–79–80
Gray, William 1943

Green, Brad 1979
Green, Edward 1923–24
Green, Max 1940
Greene, Paul 1920–21
Greenwood, Charles D. 1952–53–54
Griffith, Charles E. 1954
Griffith, Homer 1930–31–32
Grissum, James W. 1968–70
Gueguett, Dan 1903–04
Gunn, James 1967–68–69
Gurasich, Walt 1956–57
Gutierrez, Ed 1976–77

H

Haas, Earl E. 1936
Hachten, Boyd 1948
Haddock, H. 1895
Haden, Patrick C. 1972–73–74
Haigler, Charles 1905–06–07–08
Haigler, Chester 1905–06
Halderman, Richard 1927
Hall, Frank 1954–55–56
Hall, Robert H. 1929–30–31
Hall, William King 1933–34
Hall, Willie 1970–71
Halloway, Clayton 1914–15
Haluchak, Michael A. 1968–1969–70
Halvorsen, Ray 1936
Hamilton, Tom 1948
Hamilton, William 1904–05
Hamilton, Wright 1917
Hammack, Harold 1929–30–31
Han, Harold K. 1952–53
Hancock, Mike 1972–73
Hanes, Simeon 1914
Hansch, H.J. 1924
Hansen, Owen L. 1935–36–37
Hardy, Donald 1943–44–46
Hardy, James 1942–43–44
Harlan, David 1932–33
Harper, Hueston 1932–33–34
Harper, Michael 1980
Harris, Lou 1970–71
Hartwig, Carter 1976–77–78
Harvey, Clarence 1945
Hasen, H. 1902
Haslam, R. 1896
Hatch, William 1908
Hatfield, Harold 1948–49–50
Hattig, Bill 1950–51–52
Hawkins, John 1922–23–24
Hawkins, William 1930
Hawthorne, Addison 1952–53
Hayes, Jim 1952–53
Hayes, Luther 1958–59–60
Hayes, Michael 1977–79
Hayhoe, Jerry 1964–66
Hayhoe, William 1967–68
Headley, Blake 1944
Heinberg, Sylvester 1945
Heiser, Bert H. 1924–26–27
Heller, Ronald M. 1962–63–64
Henderson, James 1935–36
Hendren, Robert 1946–47–48
Henke, Edgar 1948
Henry, Michael D. 1956–57–58
Hershberger, Lloyd 1924–25–26
Hertel, Robert A. 1975–76–77
Hester, Orie 1917–19–21
Heywood, Ralph 1941–42–43
Hibbs, Gene 1935–36–37
Hibbs, Jesse 1926–27–28
Hickman, Don 1955–56–57
Hickman, Donnie J. 1974–75–76
Hicks, Harry 1923
Higgins, Clark 1944
Hill, Arthur 1909–10
Hill, Frederick G. 1962–63–64
Hill, Gary 1962–63–64
Hill, Hillard 1956–58
Hill, Jesse T. 1928–29
Hindley, Lewis 1940
Hinman, C.J. 1893–96–97
Hinton, Charles 1971–72
Hipp, Eric 1979–80
Hoff, Cecil Wayne 1927–28–29
Hoffman, Robert 1937–38–39
Hogan, Douglas J. 1973–74–75
Holden, Clark 1957–58–59
Holland, Bill 1970–71
Holman, William 1902
Holmes 1917–18
Homan, James D. 1965–66
Hooks, Robert Joseph 1951–52
Hooks, Roger C. 1954
Hoover, Phillip Lynn 1961–62
Houck, Hudson 1963
Houlgate, Jack W. 1933
Howard, Bill 1957
Howard, William N. 1933–34–35
Howell, Mike 1975

Howell, Pat 1976–77–78
Hubby, Lindsy 1956–57
Hudson, Tyrone L. 1969–70
Hughes, Don 1944–47–49
Hughes, Jack 1904–05
Hughes, John 1923
Hull, Michael 1965–66–67
Hull, Warren Bruce 1934–35
Humenuik, Rod 1956–57–58
Hummell, Edward 1910
Hunnicut 1918
Hunt 1917
Hunt, Loran J. 1961–62–63
Hunter, Floyd William III 1965
Hunter, Herbert 1917–18
Hunter, James 1978–79–80
Hunter, Keith 1921
Hurst, Joe 1933–34
Huyck, Harold 1916

I

Ickles, Sydney 1908–09
Ingle, Ray J. 1943
Isaacson, Robert 1954–55–56
Isenhouser, Bill 1919–20
Isherwood, Ed 1956–57

J

Jackson, Melvin 1974–75
Jackson, Vic 1976
Jacobsmeyer, Walter 1942
James, George 1914
Jamison, Dick 1942
Jaroncyk, William 1966–67
Jensen, Robert 1930
Jensen, Robert A. 1968–69
Jesse, John P. 1936–37–38
Jessup, Bill 1948–50
Jeter, Gary M. 1973–74–75–76
Johnson, C.J. 1904
Johnson, Dennis 1977–78–79
Johnson, Eddie 1971–72
Johnson, Gary B. 1960–61
Johnson, Kendrick 1916
Johnson, Paul Richard 1964–65
Johnson, Ricky 1977–79
Johnson, Thomas Ansley 1962–63
Johnston, E. 1918
Johnston, Rex 1956–57–58
Jones, A.E. 1889
Jones, Bob 1939–40–41
Jones, Don 1960
Jones, Ernie F. 1961–62–63
Jones, Herbert 1915
Jones, James 1936–37–38
Jones, James A. 1969–70–71
Jones, James Randy 1962
Jones, Philo 1895–96
Jordan 1917
Jordan, Frank 1977–78
Jorgenson, Ellwood 1932–34–35
Joslin, J. 1917
Joslin, J. Howard 1929–30–31
Jurich, Anthony 1929–32

K

Kaer, Morton 1924–25–26
Kalinich, Pete 1939
Kamana, John 1980
Kaprillian, Michael 1910
Kasten, Donald L. 1958
Keehn, Ludwig, 1956
Keller, Stewart 1909–10
Keller, Donald W. 1936–37
Keller, John Theron 1935
Kellogg 1917
Kelly, Fred 1914–15–16
Kemp, Rockwell 1927–28–29
Kerr, Rob 1977–78–79
Khasigian, Harry 1967–68–69
Kidder, Allan 1934–35
Kincaid, Howard 1920–21–22
King, Arthur 1921
King, Eddie Lawrence 1963–65–66
King, Marty 1977–78
King, Oscar 1922
Kirby, Jack 1946–47–48
Kirkland, Al 1952
Kirner, Gary 1962-63
Kissinger, Ellsworth H. Jr. 1954–55–56
Klein, Robert O. 1966–67–68
Klenk, Quentin 1939–40
Knickrehm, Fred W. 1917
Knoles, Tully 1901–02
Knutson, Steven C. 1973–74
Koch, Desmond 1951–52–53
Kordich, John 1948
Kovac, Pete 1934
Kraintz, Rudy 1934

Kranz, Douglas 1955–56
Kreiger, William Karl 1927–28–29
Kroll, Darrell 1942
Krueger, Al 1938–39–40
Kubas, John C. 1957
Kuchel, Theodore 1921
Kuhn, Gil 1934–35–36
Kurtak, Wayne 1954–56
Kurte, Alfred 1910

L

Laisne, Eugene 1927–28
LaMont, Grant 1925
Lane, R.C. 1904–05
Langley, Lawrence 1935–36
Lansdell, Grenville Jr. 1937–38–39
Lapka, Myron 1977–78–79
Laraneta, Manuel 1924–25–26
Lardizabel, Benjamin 1945–56–57*
Larrabee, Duane 1933–34
Lary, George 1932–33–34
LaVelle, Leslie 1926–27
Lavender, Tim 1978
Lavoni 1905
Lawrence, James D. 1966–67–68
Lawryk, Eugene 1976
Leadingham, John 1918–19–20–21
Leahy, Ed 1920–21–22
Learned 1917
LeDue, William P. 1936
Lee, Bob 1924–25–26
Lee, James 1972
Lee, Junior 1974–75
Lee, Phillip N. 1964–65–66
Lefebvre, Henry 1923–24–25
Lehmer, Steven 1967–68–69
Leimbach, Charles V. 1954–55–56
Lennox, Walter 1904
Leon, Richard G. 1966
Levingston, Robert W. 1959–60
Lewis, David R. 1974–75–76
Lewis, Mike 1958
Lilywhite, Verl 1945–46–47
Limahelu, Chris 1973–74
Lindley, Logan 1920–21–22
Lindley, Lowell 1920–21–22
Linehan, Tony 1946–47–49
Lingenfelter, Dean 1973
Littlejohn, Leroy 1942
Livernash, Leonard 1911–12–13–14–15
Lloyd, David 1944–47–48
Lockett, Frank 1919–20–21
Lockwood, John 1964–65
Logie, Dale J. 1974–75
Lopez, Frank Raymond 1964–65
Lorch, Karl 1972
Lorentzon 1907
Lott, Ron 1977–78–79–80
Loustalot, John 1923
Love, Robert 1932–33
Lowell, Russell 1947
Lubisich, Peter 1961–62–63
Lucas, Al 1920–21
Lucas, James S. 1974
Lucas, Lawrence 1914
Lucas, Pete 1917
Lund, Lavalle 1912–13–14
Lupo, Thomas Lee 1962–63–64
Lynch, Ford 1934–35–36

M

McArthur, Gary 1969
McCabe, Hilton 1926–27–28
McCaffrey, Robert A. 1972–73–74
McCall, Donald C. 1965–66
McCall, Fred 1941–42–46–47
McCardle, Mickey 1942–43–46–47
McCaslin, Lawrence 1926–27–28
McClanahan, Bob 1980
McConnell, Stephen R. 1968
McCool, Pat 1980
McCormick, Walt 1945–46–47
McCullouch, Earl R. 1967
McDonald, Mike 1976–77–78–79
McDonald, Paul 1977–78–79
McFarland, Don 1954–55
McGarvin, Tom 1940
McGee, Bob 1950
McGinley, Francis 1931–32–34
McGinn, John 1944–45
McGirr, Mike 1971–73
McGrew, Larry 1977–78–79
McKay, John K. 1972–73–74
McKeever, Marlin 1958–59–60
McKeever, Mike 1958–59–60
McKinney, Harry 1944–45–46–47

*Not a typographical error.
Lardizabel lettered in two decades.

McMahon, Richard Jr. 1961–62–63
McMillan, Walter Dan 1917–19
McMoore, Robert 1935
McMurty, Paul 1949–50
McNeil, Don 1936–37–38
McNeill, Rod 1970–72–73
McNeish, George 1934–35–36
McNeish, Robert 1931–32–33
McPartland, Kevin 1976
MacKenzie, Doug 1980
MacPhail, Peter 1941–42–43
Maddux, James 1955
Magner, Gary 1965–66–67
Malcolm, John 1908–09–10
Malette, Frank 1915–16–17
Malley, Duane 1941
Mallory, Thomas 1929–30–31
Maloney, Al 1930
Manker, Robert 1923
Manlove, Ferdinand 1925
Manning, Dick 1941
Maples, Jim 1959–60–61
Marderian, Gregory 1971–73–74
Marinovich, Andrew 1943
Marinovich, Marvin 1959–61–62
Marks, Theodore 1915–16
Marshall, G. 1915
Martin, A. 1897
Martin, G. 1895
Martin, Harry Lee 1893
Martin, Roderick D. 1975–76
Martin, William 1948
Marx, Theodore 1915–16
Marxen, E. 1915
Matthews, Bruce 1980
Matthews, Clay 1974–75–76–77
Matthews, Garland 1932–33–34
Matthews, Robert 1933–34
Mattson, Don W. 1956–57
Maudlin, Tom 1957–58
May, Reginald 1965–66
Mena, Salvador 1938–39–40
Merk, Ernest J. 1954–55
Mietz, Roger 1958–59–60
Miller 1917
Miller, John C. 1953–54–55
Miller, Reed 1902–03–04–05
Miller, Rick 1976
Miller, Robert Raymond 1966–67–68
Miller, Ronald W. 1951–52–53
Milton, John 1921–22
Mitchell, Dale 1972–73–74
Mitchell, Sheppard 1903
Mix, Ronald J. 1957–58–59
Mohler, Orville 1930–31–32
Mollett, Gerald 1959
Moloney, Jerry J. 1950
Monson, Jim 1948
Montgomery, Marvin 1969–70
Moore, James Dennia 1965–66
Moore, Kenney 1978–79–80
Moore, Malcolm 1980
Moore, Manfred 1971–72–73
Morgan, Boyd F. 1936–37–38
Morgan, David J. 1959–60–61
Morgan, Michael 1970–71
Morill, Charles 1938–39–40
Morovick, Dan 1979
Morris, Patrick J. 1975
Morris, Robert 1944
Morrison, Robert 1932
Mort, C.E. 1894–95–96
Mortensen, Jesse 1928–29
Morton, A.O. 1895
Mosebar, Don 1979–80
Moseley, Corliss C. 1915
Moser, James 1925–26–27
Moses, Charlie 1978
Moses, Don 1927–28–29
Moton, David 1963–64–65
Mullins, Gerald B. 1969–70
Munch, Arlo W. 1934
Munoz, Anthony 1976–77–78–79
Murieta, Alfred John 1886–87–88–89
Murphy, George 1944–46–47–48
Murray, Phillip 1915–16
Murray, Thomas 1934
Musick, Billie 1941
Musick, Bob 1941–42–45
Musick, James 1929–30–31
Musick, John Elmore 1944–45–46

N

Nason, Craig 1923
Naumu, Johnny 1946
Naumu, Sol 1950
Nave, Sam Doyle 1937–38–39
Neidhardt, David 1929
Neighbors, Sid 1910
Nelsen, William K. 1960–61–62
Newerf, Kenneth 1923

Newman, P.H. 1893–94–95
Newman, Wallace 1922–23–24
Nicholson, J. 1905–06
Nickoloff, Thomas 1951–52–53
Nix, Jack 1948
Nix, Lloyd 1915–16
Noble, Bill 1941–42
Noor, Dennis 1936–37
Nordstrom, Ron 1951
Norene, George 1930–31
Norris, Neil 1930–31–32
Norton, Francis 1928
Norton, Miles A. 1936–37
Nunis, Dick 1951–52
Nunnally, Lawrence 1975

O

Obbema, Joseph J. 1968
Obradovich, James R. 1973–74
Obradovich, Steve 1976
O'Brovac, Nick 1950
Ochoa, Juan 1905
O'Dell 1920
Odom, Ricky 1976–77
Oertley, Bernard 1915
Oertly, George 1917–18
Oestreich, Newell 1946
O'Grady, Steve 1977
Olivarria, Tony 1979
Oliver, Ralph 1966–67
O'Malley, John Patrick 1968
Orcutt, Gary R. 1969
Orsatti, Vic 1925–26
Ortega, Anthony S. 1956–57–58
Ossowski, Theodore L. 1943
Ostling, Gerald 1933–34
Oudermeulen, Henry 1924–25
Owens, James 1931–33

P

Packard, David 1932
Packer, Holmes 1919
Packman 1918
Page, Charles M. 1943
Page, Mike 1957
Page, Otis 1976–77–78
Page, Toby 1966–67
Palmer 1917
Palmer, Ford 1930–31–32–33
Papadakis, John 1970–71
Pappas, Nick 1935–36–37
Parker, Artimus 1971–72–73
Parsons, Charles 1903–04
Parsons, Earle O. 1943
Patapoff, William 1943
Patrick, Douglas 1964–65
Paulin, Harold 1908–09–10
Pavich, Frank R. 1952–53–54
Peake, Crawford 1925
Peccianti, Angelo 1936–38
Pehar, John 1944
Pekarcik, Al 1972
Peoples, Robert 1938–39–40
Perrin, Jay 1947
Perry 1918
Persinger, Gerald D. 1958
Peters, Ray 1978
Peters, Volney 1948–50
Peterson, Chuck 1948
Petrill, Larry N. 1965–66
Petty, Dick W. 1952–53
Peviani, Bob 1950–51–52
Phelps, Arthur 1923
Phillips, Charles W. 1972–73–74
Phillips, Floyd 1939–40
Phillips, Victor 1925
Piersen, Mel 1947
Pinckert, Erny 1929–30–31
Pitman, George 1894
Pivaroff, Ivan G. 1960–61
Plaehn, Alfred 1930–31–32
Porter, Don C. 1892
Porter, John 1927–28
Porter, Vincent 1942
Potter, Gary M. 1962
Poulsen, Alfred 1933
Powell, Edward 1972–73–74
Powell, Marvin 1974–75–76
Powers, Jim 1947–48–49
Powers, W. Russell 1934
Pranevicius, John 1940–41
Pratt, P.B. 1897
Preininger, Joe E. 1934–35–36
Premo, William 1895
Preston, Rob 1978–79
Preston, Ron 1970
Propst, Cliff 1933–34–35
Prukop, Al B. 1958–59–60
Pryor, David 1979–80
Psaltis, David (Jim) 1951–52

Pucci, Edward H. 1951–52–53
Pucci, Ralph 1948–49–50
Pugh, Allen 1977–78–80
Pultorak, Steven 1970
Purcell, James 1921–22–23
Pye, Ernest Lee 1962–63–64
Pythian, Hayden 1922–23–24

R

Radovich, Bill A. 1935–36–37
Rakhshani, Vic 1978–79–80
Rae, Michael 1970–71–72
Ramey, Theron 1930
Randle, Ken 1974–75–76
Ransom, Walt 1978
Rapp, Vivian 1914–16
Ratliff, John R. 1961–62–63
Ray, Terrel Len 1968
Rayburn, Gordon 1924
Rea, John 1945–46–47
Reade, Lynn Del 1962
Reagan, Patrick A. 1956–57
Reboin, Al 1932–33–34
Redding, William C. 1968–69
Reece, Daniel L. 1973–74–75
Reed, Dick 1945
Reed, Robert W. 1936–37
Renison, William T. 1964
Rhames, Timothy C. 1973–74–75
Rice, Carleton 1923
Richman, Denis A. 1964
Riddle, John 1922–23–24
Riddle, William Lee 1951–52–53
Ridings, Gene 1931–32–33
Rightmire, Harold 1918
Riley, Arthur 1973–74
Riley, Steve 1972–73
Rimes, Robert 1902
Ritchey, Bart 1928–30
Roberson, Theodore E. 1973–74–75
Roberts, C.R. 1955–56
Roberts, Gene 1935
Robertson, Robert 1939–40–41
Robertson, Wilbur 1949
Robinson, John 1919–20–21
Robinson, Mike 1976
Robinson, T.W. 1889–92
Rodeen, Don 1934–35
Rodriguez, Ray 1972–73
Rogers, Don 1948
Rogers, Ed 1934
Rollinson, Bruce 1971
Romer, Marshall 1943–44–46
Roquet, Russel 1940
Rorison, James 1934–35–36
Rose, Mason 1935
Rosenberg, Aaron 1931–32–33
Rosendahl, Robert A. 1956
Rosin, Benjamin L. 1959–60–61
Rossetto, John 1946
Rossovich, Timothy J. 1965–66–67
Roundy, Jay 1947–48–49
Rubke, Karl J. 1955–56
Runyon, George O. 1902–03–04
Runyon, John 1902–03–04
Ruppert, Richard 1970
Rusenhhaupt, Theodore 1908
Russell, Lynman H. 1936–37
Russo, Sam 1923
Ryan, Michael 1970–71–72
Ryan, Richard 1927
Ryus 1899

S

Saenz, Edwin M. 1943
Sagouspe, Larry 1962–63
Sahlberg, Ted 1925
Salata, Paul 1944–46–47
Salness, Ty Alwin 1964–66–67
Sampson, Ben 1950–51–52
Sampson, Vernon G. 1953–54–55
Samuels, James W. 1960
Sanbrano, Albert 1950–51
Sanchez, Armando Raul 1962–63
Sanders, Robert H. 1934–35–36
Sangster, William 1937–38–39
Sargent, Hugh 1941
Saunders, Russell 1927–28–29
Scarpace, Michael 1965–66–67
Schabre, Gus 1922
Schaube, Alvin 1926–27–28
Scheving, Albert 1925–26–27
Schindler, Ambrose 1936–37–39
Schmidt, Dennis G. 1962
Schmidt, Henry 1955
Schneider, Dean 1949–51
Schuhmacher, John 1976–77
Schute, Eugene 1905–06–07
Schutte, George 1946–47–48
Scoggins, Eric 1977–78–79–80

Scott, Daniel Blaine 1966–67–68
Scott, Joe 1960
Scott, Walter 1923–24–25
Scott, Willard 1967–68–69
Sears, James H. 1950–51–52
Seitz, William 1928–29
Seixas, John 1932–33
Seixas, William 1942
Sellers, Leon 1951–52–53
Selph, Ewald 1909
Sentous, Frank 1918
Seymore, Joseph 1902–03
Shannon, Kenneth 1932–33
Shannon, Tim 1980
Shaputis, Bob 1973
Shaver, Gaius (Gus) 1929–30–31
Shaw, Gerald 1967–68–69
Shaw, Jesse 1928–29–30
Shaw, Nathaniel 1964–65–66
Shea, Pat 1960–61
Shell, Joe 1937–38–39
Sheppard 1916
Sherman, Rodney Jarvis 1964–65–66
Sherman, Thomas Bert 1931
Shields, Alan 1959–60
Shindler, George 1921
Shipp, Joe 1977
Shuey, Edward 1935
Sigler, John 1916
Simmons, Jeff 1980
Simmrin, Randall D. 1975–76–77
Simpson, Edward 1915–16–19
Simpson, Orenthal James (O.J.) 1967–68
Sims, James 1972–73
Single, Forrest 1910
Skiles, John 1970–71
Skinner, J. 1907
Skvarna, Carl 1960–61
Slatter, James 1937–38–39
Slough, Greg C. 1969–70
Smedley, Ronald 1961–62
Smith, Ben 1893
Smith, C.E. 1895
Smith, Charles 1889–92
Smith, Dennis 1977–78–79–80
Smith, Ernest 1930–31–32
Smith, George 1925
Smith, Harry E. 1937–38–39
Smith, Herbert 1917
Smith, J.R. 1892
Smith, James 1918–19–20–21
Smith, James H. Sr. 1918–19–20–21
Smith, Jeff 1964–65
Smith, Joe W. 1923–24
Smith, Lawrence E. 1969–70
Smith, Michael W. 1973–74
Smith, R. 1910
Smith, Robert 1934
Smith, Roy 1954
Smith, S. 1918
Smith, Sidney 1968–69
Smith, Stanley 1932
Smutz, Huber 1923
Snow, James Carter 1966–67–68
Snyder, Ed N. 1937
Snyder, James 1947
Sogge, Steve 1967–68
Sohn, Ben 1938–39–40
Solter, Andrew Ford 1923–24
Sovers, Glenn 1950
Sparling, Raymond 1930–31–32
Spector, Irwin 1953–54
Speer 1916
Sperling, Ty 1977–78–79
Spraggins, Edward 1934
Sprott, C.W. 1914
Stall, Joseph 1946
Stanley, Ralph 1936–37–38
Stare, Jim 1904
Stark, Newton Calvin 1923–24–25
Stearn 1919
Steele, Harold C. 1975–76
Stephens, Barry 1929–30–31
Stephenson, Warren 1960–61
Steponovich, Tony Andrew 1927–28–29
Stevens, Lawrence 1931–32–33
Stevenson, Edward 1936
Stever, Bill 1924
Stewart, George W. 1973–74
Stewart, Melvin 1919
Stillwell, Bob 1947–48–49
Stillwell, Don 1950–51–52
Stirling, Robert 1970–71
Stoecker, Howard 1937–38–39
Stonebraker, John S. 1938–39
Stookey, Byron 1906–07–09–10
Streelman, Brad 1978–79
Strozier, Clint 1975–76
Stuart 1916
Stuart, Melvin 1919
Studdard, Howard 1977
Summer 1918

Acknowledgements
The publisher wishes to thank the following people and organizations whose inspiration, time, and thought helped make CONQUEST possible: Norman Blank; William L. Davis; Hank Erlich; Robert Gaston; Larry Kent; The Pasadena Tournament of Roses Association, Inc.; John P. Reiner; The University of Southern California — Geoff Gilchrist, Associate Vice-President, University Affairs and Executive Director of the USC General Alumni Association; Leonard Wines, Associate Vice-President, University Affairs; Dr. Richard H. Perry, Director of Intercollegiate Athletics; Jim Perry, Sports Information Director; Tim Tessalone, Sports Information Assistant; Michael Walling, Santa Monica Bank. And, a special tribute to a friend of ours and of USC's football teams, General of the Army Omar Nelson Bradley (1893-1981).

A Note on the Text
To avoid confusion, whenever co-author John Robinson is a character in the text, other than the introduction, he is referred to in the third person. Text, headlines, and photo captions referring to Robinson's tenure were written by Joe Jares and David Boss, and were approved by the coach.

Photographers
David Boss: 1, 89
Malcolm Emmons: 56, 57, 62, 122–123, 136, 139, 144a, 144b, 146, 147, 154, 156a, 156b, 157
James F. Flores: 5, 46–47, 48, 49, 50, 52–53, 53a, 55, 58, 70, 96, 97a–c, 98a, 99a–c, 100a, 100–101, 101a–f, 102–103, 105–106a, 106–107, 110, 111, 112, 113a–c, 114–115, 117, 118a, 118b, 118–119, 121a, 130a, 130b, 131, 133, 143
LIFE Picture Service: 42, 83
George Long: 6, 10, 46, 54, 63, 66–67, 94–95, 95a, 98b, 113d, 115, 121b, 126, 127, 129b, 132–133, 134, 135, 136–137, 149, 155a, 162
Richard Mackson: 64, 141, 151a–d, 153a, 158, 159a, 159b, 160–161, 161a
Peter Read Miller: 8, 13, 59, 60, 65, 66a, 68, 104, 118c, 128, 129a, 138, 140, 145, 152, 153b, 155b, 160a
Darryl Norenberg: 14, 44, 45, 61, 88, 109, 116, 124, 125
Notre Dame University: 72
Sports Illustrated: 148, 150
UCLA: 80, 81
United Press International: 27, 39, 85, 90–91
USC: 16, 18, 20, 22, 23, 24, 25, 28, 32, 34, 35a, 35b, 36, 37, 38, 40, 41, 43, 69, 86–87, 92–93, 108a, 142–143
Leigh Wiener: 30, 51
The hand-colored photographs appearing in the Heritage and Players sections of this book were tinted by Kristin Sundbom.

176